Forty Days in the Jungle

Mat Youkee has lived in Colombia since 2010, working as a freelance journalist and professional investigator. He has covered Indigenous-rights issues in Colombia, Panama, Chile, and Argentina for *The Guardian*. His reporting has also appeared in *The Economist*, *The Telegraph*, *The Financial Times*, *Americas Quarterly*, *Foreign Policy*, and other local and international publications.

T0349074

FORTY DAYS IN THE JUNGLE

Behind the Extraordinary Survival and Rescue
of Four Children Lost in the Amazon

MAT YOUKEE

SCRIBE

Melbourne | London | Minneapolis

Scribe Publications
18–20 Edward St, Brunswick, Victoria 3056, Australia
2 John St, Clerkenwell, London, WC1N 2ES, United Kingdom
3754 Pleasant Ave, Suite 100, Minneapolis, Minnesota 55409, USA

Published by Scribe 2025

Typeset by the publishers in Adobe Caslon Pro

Printed and bound in the UK by CPI Group (UK) Ltd, Croydon CR0 4YY

Scribe is committed to the sustainable use of natural resources and the
use of paper products made responsibly from those resources.

978 1 761380 91 4 (Australian edition)
978 1 915590 79 4 (UK edition)
978 1 957363 95 0 (US edition)
978 1 761385 93 3 (ebook)

Catalogue records for this book are available from the
National Library of Australia and the British Library.

scribepublications.com.au
scribepublications.co.uk
scribepublications.com

Contents

Part III: The Children of the Jungle

To the children of the jungle

Author's Note

In the late afternoon of June 9, 2023, there was a sudden salvo of horns from the cars on Bogotá's gridlocked streets. The motorists' celebration, the standard response to a goal by Colombia's national soccer team, came in response to a breaking-news radio bulletin. Forty days after their plane had disappeared over the remote jungle in the south of the country, four Indigenous children had been found alive by rescuers.

It was a cathartic moment, and an unexpected one. Three weeks previously, the plane, Cessna HK-2803, had been discovered with its nose down, its tail in the air, as upright as the broad trees that surrounded it. The bodies of the three adults on board had been identified, but the children were nowhere to be found. Colombians tuned in to the nightly news for updates on the massive search-and-rescue operation. They were introduced to a cast of characters that seemed to come straight from a *telenovela*. There were anguished fathers and telepathic grandmothers, baffled commandos and wizened shamans, treacherous jungle spirits and a heroic Belgian shepherd called Wilson. But by the time May slid into June, the prospect of the children's survival had all but vanished, and many Colombians had given up hope of a happy ending.

I shared their pessimism. Having spent a decade living in and writing about Colombia, I had become cautious about any so-called good news. Too often, the country's 48 million inhabitants had seen unexpected successes or hard-fought victories undermined by tragedy or farce. Economic booms were swiftly extinguished by financial crises. Popular and charismatic political leaders were almost invariably exposed as corrupt. Guerrillas and paramilitary groups would surrender, only for new ones to take their place. Colombia's remote rural populations—in particular, its eighty-seven Indigenous groups—always seemed to bear the brunt of such ill fortune.

When the news broke on X (formerly Twitter) that the children had been rescued, I was overjoyed. Within five minutes I had shot off an email to my editor at *The Guardian* asking to report the story, and in the days that followed I would file several more articles, scraped together from whatever new information was available, to meet huge international media interest in the children's story. I was invited to video in my thoughts for UK chat shows and Australian radio networks, and my inbox filled with requests from documentary filmmakers requesting my help to speak to the children and their families. In Colombia, it was the biggest story of the year.

But just as global interest in the story reached its peak, a veil of silence fell. Following a month in hospital, the children entered the custody of the child-welfare services, where they remain at the time of writing. A year after the event, Lesly, the oldest child, gave a brief account of their time in the jungle to investigators seeking to determine the cause of the crash. The only other sources of information were family members who had visited the children, and members of the rescue teams. These accounts were vague and often contradictory. Many questions remained unanswered.

Before it was a survival story, the fate of HK-2803 and its passengers had the trappings of a mystery. As the jumbled, misspelled names of the children on board were published by Colombia's Civil Aviation Authority, the identity of the family and the reasons for their travel became the focus of idle curiosity. In the wake of the children's rescue, the questions seemed to multiply. *Who were the family? Why were they travelling? Why did it take the rescue team so long to find them? How did they survive?*

I decided to write this book out of a desire to find answers to these questions. In late 2023 and early 2024, I made several trips to the Colombian Amazon to speak to the friends and families of the passengers, and the soldiers and Indigenous volunteers who had participated in the search. This was not always an easy process. Along the banks of the Caquetá River, an atmosphere of fear meant that people couldn't always speak freely, and some requested that their names be omitted. Often, the stories they told were not happy ones. There were family feuds, betrayals, accusations, and threats. But in my conversations I was advised— and occasionally admonished—to tell the *real* story, the deeper historical and political circumstances that shaped the fate of HK-2803 and its passengers.

From the start of my research, I had an inkling that behind the happy miracle of the children's survival, their story held wider, hard truths about the realities faced by the inhabitants of the Colombian Amazon. The Indigenous people of the region live in poverty, under the shadow of armed groups, their culture eroded by extractive businesses, and their needs neglected by the state. I suspected that the spotlight shone on the region in the summer of 2023 would only briefly highlight the importance of preserving Indigenous culture before panning away. The conditions that created the disaster would remain unaddressed.

During my research, I spoke to anthropologists, historians, human rights activists, and security analysts. But I wanted to base as much of the story as possible on the words and actions of those closest to the children, and those involved in the search. Where there are conflicting accounts, I had to use my own judgment to attempt to untangle the truth, or, failing that, clarify the areas of disagreement and doubt for the reader to decide. I have done my best to identify the most likely actions and motivations of the children in the jungle without speculating too heavily on their inner thoughts. In recognition of the unavoidable element of creative license involved, these chapters are represented in a different font.

Cast of Characters

Puerto Sábalo & Chukiki

Magdalena Mucutuy: Uitoto mother to Lesly, Soleiny, Tien, and Cristin, as well as Angie and John Andrés

Andrés Jacobombaire: Magdalena's first husband (married 2008)

Angie Jacobombaire Mucutuy (b. 2007): First daughter of Andrés & Magdalena

Lesly Jacobombaire Mucutuy (b. 2009): Second daughter of Andrés & Magdalena

John Andrés Jacobombaire Mucutuy (b. 2012): Son of Andrés & Magdalena

Soleiny Jacobombaire Mucutuy (b. 2014): Third daughter of Andrés & Magdalena

Narciso Mucutuy: Magdalena's father

Maria Fatima Mucutuy: Magdalena's mother

Fidencio Mucutuy: Narciso's brother, Magdalena's uncle

Manuel Miller Ranoque: Magdalena's boyfriend

Tien Noriel Ranoque Mucutuy (b. 2019): Son of Manuel & Magdalena

Cristin Neriman Ranoque Mucutuy (b. 2022): Daughter of Manuel & Magdelena

William Castro: Childhood friend of Manuel Ranoque,
  governor of Puerto Sábalo (2023)
Diana Rodríguez: Magdalena's childhood friend, displaced to
  Bogotá
Adelia Rotieroke: Magdalena's godmother, resident of La
  Chorrera

The Mendoza family
Herman Mendoza: Indigenous rights defender, passenger on
  HK-2803
Delio Mendoza: Herman's younger brother and Amazonian
  researcher, member of the Araracuara search team
Ismael Mendoza: Father of Herman and Delio, former guard at
  Araracuara prison
Diana Mendoza: Younger sister of Herman and Delio, organizer
  of the search team

Avianline pilots and search team
Hernando Murcia: Pilot of flight HK-2803
Fredy Ladino: Owner of Avianline Charters
Harry Castañeda: Avianline pilot
José Miguel Calderón: Bush pilot, former colleague of Hernando
  Murcia
Ferney Garzón: Member of the Avianline search team
Andrés Londoño: Member of the Avianline search team
Florencio Tamborrero: Resident of Cachiporro and member of
  Avianline search team

Special Operations Combined Command (CCOES)
General Pedro Sánchez: Commander of the CCOES
Captain Edwin Montiel: Leader of Dragon 4 Team

Sergeant Wilmer Miranda: Second-in-command of Dragon 4
Team

Lieutenant Juan Felipe Montoya: Leader of Destroyer 1 Team

Sergeant Juan Carlos Rojas: Second-in-command of Destroyer 1
Team

Captain Armando Guerrero: Head of logistics for Operation
Hope

Araracuara

Edwin Paky: Cartographer and researcher, Herman Mendoza's
second cousin

Henry Guerrero: Member of the Araracuara volunteer search
team, teacher

Nestor Andoke: Member of the Araracuara volunteer search
team, hunter

Serafina Guerrero: Matriarch of Guerrero family, preparer of
yagé

Martha Muñoz: Owner of the town shop

Superintendent Jeison Castro: Police officer on duty in
Araracuara

Santiago Buraglia: Consultant for Yauto, a carbon-bond
company

Puerto Leguízamo

José Rubio Rodríguez: Medicine man

Elíecer Muñoz: Member of Puerto Leguízamo search team

Nicolás Ordóñez: Member of Puerto Leguízamo search team

Dairo Kumariteke: Member of Puerto Leguízamo search team

Edwin Manchola: Member of Puerto Leguízamo search team

Glossary

agua panela: a warm drink made from brown sugarcane

ambil: a liquid tobacco widely used by the People of the Center

barbasco: a tree root containing mild toxins used to stun fish in lagoons

cacique: the traditional leader of a tribe or clan, reserved for those with a knowledge of the history and cosmology of his people.

caguana: a traditional Amazonian juice made from pineapples

casabe: a flat bread made from grated manioc with a gelatinous core

chagra: a small plot of land cleared each year for cultivation

colono: a white settler in the jungle

copuazú: a fruit with a brown skin and white flesh related to cacao

curandero: a medicine man

duende: a shape-shifting spirit

fariña: a granola-like grain made from manioc

guácharo: a cave-dwelling Amazonian bird

lancha: a long, open-top wooden canoe powered by an outboard motor

maloca: a high-vaulted, palm-thatched ceremonial building

mambé: a green powder of coca leaves and ash consumed by men

minga: an Indigenous practice of coming together to achieve a
    common good

monte: the wild jungle that surrounds settlements

paisanos: Indigenous peoples with a common land of origin

sábalo: a large, fleshy fish native to the Colombian Amazon

sabaleta: a small fish with little meat

siringa: a latex-bearing tree

tucupi: a spicy sauce made from manioc

tupui: a flat-topped sandstone mountain

vereda: a small riverside settlement

vidente: a fortune teller

yagé: the juice from a hallucinogenic vine

PART I

MAGDALENA

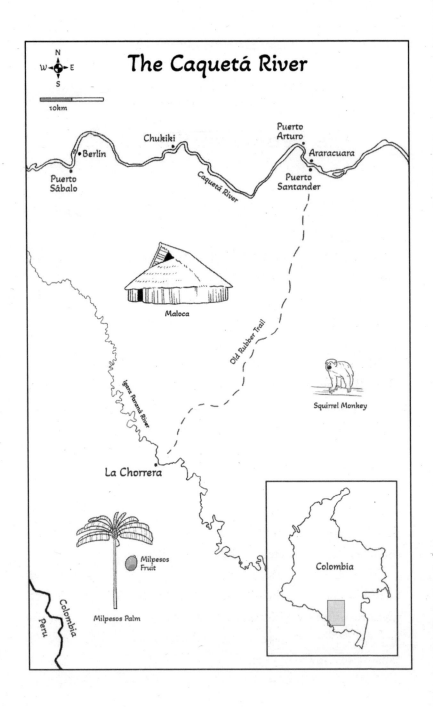

The Caquetá River

10km

Puerto Sábalo • Berlín • Chukiki • Caquetá River • Puerto Arturo • Araracuara • Puerto Santander

Maloca

Igara Paraná River

Old Rubber Trail

Squirrel Monkey

La Chorrera

Milpesos Fruit

Milpesos Palm

Colombia / Peru

Colombia

CHAPTER ONE

The People of the Center

In the early morning of Monday April 16, 2023, a boatman steered his tiny craft mid-channel, scanning the riverbank for a break in the jungle, for a tributary enclosed by an arch of branches. It was the rainy season, and the Caquetá River was running high and wide.

The jungle can be a gloomy, disorientating, and inhospitable place. But there are times of day, there are angles of perspective, when it assumes an idyllic beauty, when it can seem almost benign. This was one of those moments. The morning air was cool, and the wide sky was streaked with thin, feathery clouds. Birdsong from the distant riverbanks was the only interruption to the gentle chug of the outboard motor and the lapping of waves against the bow. From the middle of the river, the jungle was a thin fringe of green on the horizon; the trunks of the nearest trees shone white, illuminated by the low sun. Beyond them, darkness.

He rode in a *lancha,* a long, open-top wooden canoe with a forty-horsepower outboard motor affixed to the stern. At his feet was a two-liter soda bottle filled with gasoline and a bundled-up tarp for deployment against the sudden showers. In this remote expanse of the Colombian Amazon, where waterways served as roads, there are dozens of small riverside settlements, known as *veredas.* For their Indigenous populations, the lancha is a lifeline. It is the universal and versatile form of transport, assuming the role of taxicab, school bus, and delivery vehicle.

The boatman pulled on the tiller and steered towards the tributary that led to the vereda of Chukiki. Sitting on a tree stump in the shade with a couple of backpacks at her feet, Magdalena Mucutuy heard the sound of the outboard motor. She was thirty-three years old and a mother of six, but her body retained the athleticism of her youth. Her arms were slender yet muscled, with a copper tone that stood in contrast to the white of her T-shirt. Her face was lean, with prominent cheekbones and a wide, full mouth. She got to her feet and told her children to gather their things.

In her arms she held Cristin, her ten-month-old daughter by her boyfriend, Manuel Ranoque. Cristin was a robust baby, with plump forearms and shoulder-length hair, a portion of which her mother kept tied in a top knot.

Around the base of the tree, Tien and Soleiny were playing. Tien was Cristin's full brother, a boisterous, mischievous four-year-old who delighted in teasing his older sisters. People often remarked how much he reminded them of his father. Soleiny was the youngest of Magdalena's four children from a previous relationship. She was nine, talkative and full of smiles, but with a stubborn streak, particularly insistent on wearing her hair just the way she liked it, in a pair of bunches.

Two of Magdalena's children still lived with her ex-partner's family. The fourth child waiting in the shade was Lesly. Thirteen years old, but already long-limbed and strong, she was the one who most took after her mother. She was quiet and diligent, and she took her responsibility as the eldest seriously. As the prow of the lancha slid to a halt on the muddy riverbank, and the boatman, in gumboots, stepped out to tie the line, it was she who helped load the family's luggage and cover it with the tarp. It was down to her to ensure that Tien and Soleiny took their places on the wooden cross planks and stopped squabbling.

Of the children, she was the only one who understood the reason for their mother's sudden decision to leave the jungle.

As they headed out into the current of the Caquetá, Lesly watched with dark, intelligent eyes while Magdalena cradled Cristin with one arm and with the other hand scanned through the messages from Manuel on her cell phone. They were details of an escape plan. Once they reached Araracuara, an hour's trip downriver, Magdalena was to head straight to the police station in the army base and demand seats on the next flight to San José del Guaviare, a city 360 kilometers to the north. From there, they could take the overnight bus to Bogotá, the capital in the Andes, where Manuel would be waiting for them.

Magdalena had never left the jungle of southern Colombia. As the spray kicked up from the prow, she gave a final nervous glance upstream, into the gray glare of the morning sun behind clouds. She looked back towards Chukiki, the town where she had been born and where, that morning, she had said a cold goodbye to her parents. Beyond that, further upriver, lay Puerto Sábalo, the vereda she had called home for the last five years. It was where she had built a house, a farm, and a life. From her seat on the lancha, she watched this familiar stretch of the Caquetá River slip by for the last time.

William Castro recalls the day, in early 2019, when he saw his old friend Manuel Ranoque pitch up in Puerto Sábalo with a woman and three children in tow. Manuel was a burly, vigorous man, and although William hadn't seen him for many years, he'd heard rumors of his exploits. Working on the illegal mining barges that dredged for gold up and down the Caquetá, Manuel had earned a reputation for drinking and partying. The last William had heard of him, he'd been picked up by the army and thrown in jail in Leticia, the Colombian city on the border with Brazil.

Manuel seemed calmer now, more mature. He introduced William to Magdalena and her two daughters, Lesly and Soleiny. He doted on Tien, who was still a babe in arms, with the enthusiasm of a first-time father. He had come back to the place of his birth, he said, to build a house and settle down. William, a devout Catholic, was delighted by the news.

"Their arrival was good for us because they had a lot of kids," he remembers. "We were going to repopulate the community." He thought it was admirable that Manuel had assumed the responsibility for his two stepdaughters. William's mother, the local schoolteacher, was excited to have new students after years of enduring dwindling class sizes and the sorry sight of empty chairs.

William recounts all this while sitting on the floor, leaning back against the wall of his house in Puerto Sábalo. He wears gumboots and a black tank top, and his wiry frame is coated in a sheen of sweat after a day's labor digging drainage ditches. Other days are dedicated to maintenance—replacing rotting wooden panels on the houses, de-rusting the village's diesel generator, and incinerating trash. These days, shielding Puerto Sábalo from the deleterious effects of the jungle is a never-ending job, but for a period William had nurtured ambitious plans for his community.

His house is the most impressive in Puerto Sábalo, three stories tall with walls painted yellow and baby blue. There is a large television, a fridge, and a crucifix on the wall. In the afternoons, a cool breeze blows through the wide windows.

"People here tend to just build a wooden box, divide it in two, and live inside," he explains. "I wanted to do something different."

The idea was to set an example, a new tone, for the village. William had planned to make the house even bigger and more comfortable, but the building work had overrun, and the money had run out. Now he wonders what could have possessed him to undertake such an ambitious project on the banks of the Caquetá.

"It's a white elephant," he says.

For both William and Manuel, Puerto Sábalo possessed a heritage they felt a responsibility to protect. In 1932, their great-grandfathers, Uitoto employees of a white-run rubber company, had been descending the Caquetá in canoes in search of the latex-yielding *siringa* tree when they came across a long sandbank covered in ducks. They shot a few with their Winchester rifles, and when they dropped their hooks in the surrounding waters, they pulled up an impressive catch of *sábalo*, a delicious, fleshy fish.

That day lingered in the memory long after the men returned to their back-breaking jobs at the rubber company and they would often reminisce about that bend of the Caquetá River, so rich in fish and game. In the late 1960s, they hacked their way through the forest back to the remembered spot. They built a new community, naming it after the fish in the waters. It was meant to be a place where the Uitoto could live a traditional, independent existence.

During his courtship of Magdalena, Manuel had talked lovingly of his hometown and of the childhood days he had spent with his late grandfather, Puerto Sábalo's *cacique,* its leader and spiritual elder—a man who knew the mysteries of every plant in the forest and who sang the songs of his Uitoto ancestors.

However, when Magdalena followed her boyfriend to Puerto Sábalo, she found a very different place. It was home to a couple dozen families, some of whom lived in a cluster of wooden-paneled houses on stilts by the riverside, while others had made their homes at a distance, on the surrounding hill. The original *malocas*, the high-vaulted, palm-thatched ceremonial buildings that form the center of Uitoto social and spiritual life, were rotting away.

No sábalo swam in the shallows; no ducks sunned their feathers on the sandbank. The village elders grumbled that their old ways of living had been abandoned. The Indigenous population of the Amazon had once lived in harmony with the jungle. A man would go to the river to shoot a duck or spear a fish to meet his family's daily needs. In a few short years in the 1980s, however, the villagers had slaughtered the ducks and used nets to rake the waters clean of fish. The produce was sold downriver in the town of Araracuara. It was a one-time bonanza, never to be repeated, and the profits were quickly spent, leaving only hunger and division behind.

"Only the story remains," says William ruefully. "You have to be pretty good to catch a sábalo these days."

Manuel believed he could arrest his hometown's decline, and his return to Puerto Sábalo provided a jolt to the sleepy vereda. Some of the elders in the village had known him as a boy. He had been a tearaway and a troublemaker, they remembered, before he set off to look for work at the age of seventeen. Now he was twenty-seven, with a muscular frame and an apparently insatiable appetite for physical labor. William recognized a kindred spirit, a man with the energy and drive to turn the village around.

"If we sent him to dig a trench, he'd grab the shovel and off he went. He was an animal for work," he says.

With chainsaw in hand, Manuel set off into the *monte*, the wild jungle that surrounded the vereda, to cut the timber needed to build his family a new house. He raised chickens, and made a trade selling rice and cooking oil to the villagers to earn extra cash. It was a welcome injection of entrepreneurial spirit.

Less than a year after Manuel's arrival, William moved to Florencia, the capital of the department of Caquetá, and the only place where his disabled son could receive the treatment he required. When he returned to Puerto Sábalo in 2022, Manuel had built his house—two rooms built on stilts with a palm roof—and had assumed the role of the de facto leader of the community.

"He'd grown up, but he was a bit full of himself," William remembers. "Together, we formed a sort of political party. I was his adviser, his right hand. [He said] that the community needed this and that, that we needed more supplies and access to state services. He was right. Puerto Sábalo wasn't recognized by the state, we didn't have a bank account, and without them we couldn't work with the institutions."

The two men spent their evenings together at William's house. They had to acquire a pump to bring in clean water from inland sources. They needed to secure a favorable deal on gasoline for the generator. They had to pressure the relevant authorities to improve access and teaching at the local secondary schools, which lay upriver.

They agreed, too, that Puerto Sábalo needed to recapture its essence, its traditional Indigenous culture. For twenty years, the town had not had a cacique, because no one had the requisite intimate knowledge of the history and cosmology of their people. Manuel seemed determined to drag the community out of its state of lethargy, and he had a plan to do it.

Part of this plan involved signing up Puerto Sábalo to a

carbon-bond scheme. Over the course of 2022, consultants from Yauto, a Bogotá-based consultancy, paid regular visits to the community. In the maloca, they did their best to explain to the villagers how they could benefit from protecting the surrounding forest. If they could reduce the amount of jungle cut down for cattle grazing or lumber, they would earn a carbon bond that Yauto could sell to polluting companies in industrialized countries to offset their emissions.

Not everyone grasped the finer details of the United Nations' REDD+ program, but they understood that, with the money they earned, they could fund their own much-needed social projects, and that there would be enough left over for monthly payments to each villager.

Manuel intended to become the community's representative with Yauto. In December 2022, he ran for governor of Puerto Sábalo with William as his secretary. Some of the old-timers were skeptical. The governorship was an administrative position, but they believed Manuel held ambitions for a more prestigious role that he was not qualified for. "He came here, and he planted his staff in the ground, and said, 'I will be the next cacique,'" says one elder in the village.

In the event, however, no one wanted to mount any serious opposition to Manuel, and he was elected governor. In William's view, the villagers had seen a man transformed after his adolescent misdemeanors. "The community gave him the position so that he could turn over a new leaf in his life," he says. "I put a lot of trust in Manuel. A *lot* of trust."

As her boyfriend divided his time between physical labor and community politics, Magdalena performed the role of dutiful wife, although, in fact, she and Manuel had never married. In the first years, their only option was to sleep in the rundown maloca that had belonged to Manuel's grandfather. She did her best to make it a home. It had a dirt floor, but it was wide and spacious. The family's furniture—a table, a few chairs, and a large metal griddle—seemed tiny under the high roof.

In one corner of the maloca there was an open firepit over which Magdalena would cook grated manioc into *casabe*, a flat bread with a crispy exterior and a gelatinous core. Manioc, a long, brown tuber with a white, starch-rich center, is a staple of the Amazonian diet. Resistant to drought and able to grow in nutrient-poor soils, the crop has been cultivated for centuries by Indigenous civilizations. They have also developed a variety of methods—soaking, fermentation, cooking—to remove the cyanide that the tuber contains.

Magdalena grew the manioc herself. A few hundred meters from the maloca, at the end of a path that rose up the hillside and crossed streams bridged by flimsy wooden planks, lay her *chagra*, a small plot for cultivating crops and plants. Each September, Manuel would fell an area of forest with his chainsaw and then burn the branches, leaving a fertile layer of ash on the surface. Magdalena planted manioc, corn, and plantain seeds in carefully spaced rows. Throughout the year, she would weed the ground and guard the plants against plagues. Her chagra was healthy and well organized, the thin V-shaped branches of the manioc topped with thick bushes of green leaves.

More than just a source of food for her family, the chagra was a female space. If the men held forth in the maloca, the chagra was the place where the women of the community could exchange food and seeds, help each other with horticultural chores, and pass on their knowledge of plants to the younger generation.

Sometimes the chagras were located several kilometers from the village, in the monte, and it was here that girls could develop an understanding of, and a connection to, the jungle. Since childhood, it was the place where Magdalena felt most at home.

She was born in 1990, the third child of Narciso Mucuty, from the Muinane people, and Maria Fatima Valencia, a Uitoto. The Colombian Amazon is home to forty-four different Indigenous peoples, but the tribes that inhabit the basin between the Caquetá River and the Putumayo River, on the southern border with Peru, are known collectively as the People of the Center. As well as the Uitoto and Muinaine, the other major tribes are the Andoque, Bora, Ocaina, and Nonuya and, nowadays, intermarriage between these groups is the norm. Their members often refer to each other as *paisanos,* the Spanish word for "compatriots" that the Indigenous use to refer to those from their common land of origin. What links these peoples and sets them apart from neighboring Amazonian Indigenous groups are their shared cultivation and ceremonial practices.

The People of the Center also refer to themselves as the "People of Tobacco, Coca and Sweet Manioc" after the three agricultural products they hold sacred. The first is *ambil*, a dark, viscous tobacco paste that is rubbed into the tongue or gums with a finger. To the foreign palate it can taste a little like a fishy marmite, albeit with an immediate and subtle buzz, and it's easy to see why it's believed to aid dialogue and inspire intelligence and thought.

The cultivation of the tobacco used to make ambil is the exclusive preserve of the men of the community. So, too, is the growth of coca leaves, which are pulverized and added to the ashes of local trees to form *mambé,* a green powder applied to the space between the lower teeth and cheek, which the men use during their ceremonies in the maloca. Boys are taught to *mambear* by their fathers—not moistening the mambé sufficiently with saliva can lead to inhaling the powder into the lungs, resulting in coughing fits and, in extreme cases, suffocation.

The People of the Center also use a certain type of sweet manioc to make ceremonial drinks that are consumed during dances in the maloca. These dances have long been a distinctive element of the local culture. When a German anthropologist visited a Uitoto village in 1914, the tribe members told him, "We work in order to dance." Although the dress code may have changed—today young Uitotos often sport soccer shirts and sneakers—these events retain a vital role in fostering inter-tribe relations.

In Puerto Sábalo, however, such dances had become increasingly rare. In the evenings, when the village's diesel generator kicked in, families would gather in those houses on which gray satellite dishes protruded from the roof. If a soccer match wasn't on, they would watch a *telenovela* set in Bogotá, Medellín, or the Caribbean city of Cartagena. The actors were glamorous, the clothes stylish, and the settings luxurious.

Over the course of Magdalena's life, many of her friends and relatives had migrated to Bogotá. The clever ones went to study, often on scholarships, at the city's universities. Others found jobs through friends. Some had been forced to move there out of fears for their safety in the jungle.

When they returned during the holidays, they often grumbled about the capital city, 2,600 meters up in the chilly Andean mountains. They referred to it as *la nevera*, the refrigerator. They complained about the streets full of traffic, the disorientating effect of the glass and brick towers, and the unrelenting pace of life there. Finding work was hard, staying warm was impossible, and they missed the territory, the chagra, and the food. But all this was said in a self-effacing manner. Their paisanos could tell, by the clothes they wore and the cell phones they carried, that the city was also a place of opportunity.

If Magdalena had once harbored ambitions to move to the city, life had not worked out that way. She had little formal education, barely any money, children to care for, and a chagra to tend. Suddenly, however, leaving the jungle became her only option.

One night in early April 2023, Manuel Ranoque disappeared. The next morning, William Castro noticed that a lancha was missing from the riverside. Manuel had traveled through the night to reach Araracuara, and had headed straight to the police station. From there, he'd been put on an air force transport plane that same afternoon and flown out of the jungle. He'd been run out of town by armed guerrillas, he said, and now the lives of his partner and children were under threat.

CHAPTER TWO

The Left Hand

In the veredas of the Caquetá River, the paisanos will sometimes refer, often in hushed tones, to *la mano izquierda*, the left hand. The term is deliberately ambiguous, for two reasons. First, it is unwise to speak too specifically about the armed groups that prowl the banks of the Caquetá River. Second, over the last fifty years, so many guerrilla armies, drug cartels, and paramilitary gangs have infiltrated the region that it can be hard to keep up with the waxing and waning of each one's influence. In the 1960s, around the time that the Uitoto men were putting up the first buildings in Puerto Sábalo, an armed peasant uprising against Colombia's right-wing government was being consolidated into an organized rebel army.

The Revolutionary Armed Forces of Colombia (FARC) were born in the coffee hills south of Bogotá, but they soon spread east into the Amazon jungle, a natural hiding place beyond the reach of the Colombian military. In 1999, when Magdalena was nine years old, FARC fighters took control of Araracuara and the surrounding region. They were a well-organized outfit, with camouflage uniforms, AK-47 rifles, and armbands colored in the yellow, red, and blue of the Colombian flag.

In a region totally cut off from the Colombian state, many

Indigenous welcomed the semblance of order that the guerrillas provided, according to Juan Alvaro Echeverri, an anthropologist who was working in Araracuara at the time.

"Whilst the guerrillas were in charge, things worked wonderfully. In fact, people were happy," he says. "They put rules in place that anyone who stole, who got drunk, or who hit his woman would have to do hard labor, maintaining the road [in Araracuara]. That road was never in better shape."

In November 2003, however, two battalions of troops landed at the airstrip, and the first sandbags of an army base were put in place. For the next decade, the People of the Center found themselves in the crossfire as the military tried to wrestle back control of the jungle from the FARC. They would be forced to submit and cooperate by one group, only to be punished for doing so by the other. The Indigenous started to inform on each other. Paranoid guerrillas began executions. In short, says Echeverri, "everything went to shit."

So when a 2016 peace treaty between the government and the FARC was put to a referendum, the inhabitants of the department of Caquetá voted overwhelmingly for an end to the violence. Across the country, 90 per cent of FARC fighters laid down their weapons in the coming years. But the People of the Center had no such luck. In the Caquetá jungle, things played out differently.

Ivan Mordisco, the commander of the FARC's First Front, which operated in the jungles of southern Colombia, was the one senior guerrilla to defect from the peace negotiations. He claimed that his comrades had abandoned their left-wing principles. The reality was that the region he controlled, with its riverine cocaine routes and its illegal goldmining, was simply too lucrative to give up.

Clean-shaven and menacing, despite his professorial spectacles, Mordisco was a bold strategist and an elusive target. When the FARC sent their most fearsome veteran to pull him into line, Mordisco recruited him to his ranks. In July 2022, the army reported they had killed him in an air strike—but, nine months later, he showed up on Colombian TV, alive and well, brandishing an Israeli-made machine gun. The Estado Mayor Central (EMC), as his new dissident guerrilla group was known, expanded rapidly into the vacuum that the FARC had left behind.

At first, the inhabitants of Puerto Sábalo saw little change from the situation they had lived with for decades. The guerrillas conducted their business on the water and in the jungles beyond, and they rarely asked more from the paisanos than their silence. In mid-2020, however, in the midst of the Covid-19 pandemic, Magdalena and her neighbors along the Caquetá River began to receive messages from the guerrillas on their cell phones.

Like every other mother in Colombia, she was fretting about the impact this deadly new virus would have on her family. Facemasks and alcohol gel were almost impossible to find. There was no clinic capable of treating serious cases, and the nearest ventilators were thousands of kilometers away. The government had cut off flights to the region, and now food was running low.

The EMC took on the responsibilities that the state was unwilling to fulfill. Over WhatsApp, they set the rules on curfews and lockdowns. On the rivers, they established checkpoints to keep outsiders away. It was the guerrillas who provided food and loans to the vulnerable population. Mordisco united smaller dissident groups under his command, and the EMC became the de facto force in the jungle, establishing a level of control over the territory not seen since the FARC's heyday.

"During the pandemic, the EMC suddenly realized they could

openly control the territory and that nobody was going to come after them," says Sergio Saffon, a security analyst. "The Caquetá region became the birthplace of a new national project of the FARC dissidents."

From 2020 onwards, the guerrillas became an ever more frequent sight in Puerto Sábalo. Magdalena saw them come to the village to talk to the men—sometimes emerging from the jungle in olive uniforms, sometimes arriving by lancha in civilian clothes. They requested information, and settled disputes in town. But to control their expanding territory, they needed new members to boost their ranks.

News of the guerrillas' attempts to recruit Indigenous children spread down the Caquetá. Upriver parents complained that the dean of the secondary school had invited EMC members to give lectures to the students on revolutionary theory. Boys were enticed to sign up by attractive female guerrillas or by promises of wealth. From 2020 to 2022, at least twenty-one children were recruited in the Amazon region, according to local human rights groups, but the rate accelerated in 2023. In the first six months of that year, eighteen joined the ranks of armed groups.

When the children couldn't be persuaded, they were taken by force. In March 2023, an EMC leader known as *El Gato* abducted four children from an Indigenous community fifty kilometers upriver of Puerto Sábalo. Two months later, they were found dead, executed by the guerrillas after they tried to escape. Magdalena feared for Lesly, who, at thirteen, was at risk of becoming a target for recruitment. According to Manuel, Lesly told her mother that the guerrillas had approached her in February that same year.

When Manuel fled Puerto Sábalo in the middle of the night in early April, Magdalena suddenly found herself alone. She went first to her brother's house in the vereda of Berlín, and then took her children to her parents' place in Chukiki. Over the course of those five days, her relatives said she would walk among the trees, out of earshot, to talk on her cell phone. From her angry gestures and hunched shoulders, they could tell she was arguing with Manuel.

By April 16, Magdalena had reached a decision. Her family could not remain in the jungle. She had to take her children to Araracuara, and get the first flight out.

On the lancha, Magdalena watched as the river narrowed, the current swelled, and their pace accelerated. On the banks, the terrain climbed into thickly forested hills, and soon they were surrounded on both sides by gray cliffs that stretched vertically for fifty meters. Dozens of waterfalls emptied from the overhanging lips of these rock formations directly into the river below, blowing up a mist that sparkled in the sunlight.

The Caquetá is a mighty and turbulent river. It emerges in the windy, rain-soaked moorland of the Andean mountains and descends rapidly eastwards through deep valleys and gorges until it reaches the lowland plains of the Amazon Basin. There it meanders in great loops before crossing into Brazil and merging with the Amazon River, 2,800 kilometers from its source. As with Colombia's other jungle rivers, the Caquetá is punctuated with impassable rapids and waterfalls that have served to both isolate and protect the region.

Magdalena and her children were passing through a *tupui*, one of the flat-topped sandstone mountains that stand like lonely sentinels above the jungle in this part of the Amazon. The Uitotos' ancestors believed these other-worldly towers of rock to be the lairs of dangerous primordial spirits, and they had originally settled deep in the forest so as to keep a wary distance from them. In the narrow confines of the gorge, the lancha lurched from side to side as it carved its way through pockets of white water. At low tide, when the rocks were closer to the surface, this was a dangerous crossing, only attempted by the most experienced boatmen; but on this day, the lancha proceeded unscathed, emerging suddenly into a river that grew calm and widened once again.

Thirty minutes later, they reached Puerto Arturo, the port that served Araracuara. A handful of rundown but brightly colored trading boats were strung together in the tiny, shallow bay. On the muddy slipway, a team of men were loading cardboard boxes of food and crates of beer onto a trailer attached to a tractor. A white man, topless and fat under a wide-brimmed straw hat, sat at the controls. The tractor was the only vehicle hardy enough to drag the merchandise along the decrepit road. Magdalena shunned the solicitations of a couple of motorbike drivers offering rides into town. She shouldered her backpack, pulled Cristin in tight to her body, and, with her three other children beside her, began the long slog up hill.

The road was abysmal—a trench of pale, slippery clay, cut through with thin streams of water and deep potholes. For two kilometers, it snaked uphill towards the crest of another tupui, which loomed over Araracuara and the surroundings jungle.

At the summit, she led her children across the gravel runway to the army base where a large red satellite dish poked above ten-foot walls of green sandbags. By the entrance, a wooden sign carried the logo of the Bilac 50 jungle regiment: a black panther crouching over a pair of crossed rifles. Magdalena spoke to the guards, and they let her through. Inside, Superintendent Jeison Castro was expecting her.

"They walked up from the port, and she came looking for me," he recalls. "She had a baby in her arms, and three children with her. She told me that she was the partner of Ranoque and that I had to send her in a plane."

Castro is a burly veteran cop with short, gray hair. Over a long career in the Colombian police force, he had been rotated through a number of jungle postings. Araracuara, in his view, is the toughest. Once, before his time, there had been a police station in town, but now the cops were largely confined to a small office behind the protective walls of the army base.

There were many areas on his beat, especially on the other side of the river, where the police wouldn't set foot in groups of less than twenty. There were known drug routes running through the jungle just a few hundred meters away, but there were scant resources and little inclination to do anything about them. Meanwhile, the Indigenous either didn't trust the police or didn't want to risk being seen cooperating with them. There was nothing to do except hunker down in the army base and wait for the next rotation, hopefully to Leticia, the most developed city in the jungle, with its restaurants, cafés, and air conditioning. Occasionally, however, a paisano would wander into the base to file a report.

A week earlier, in the first hours of the morning, Manuel Ranoque had turned up at Superintendent Castro's desk looking wet and tired. He told the policeman that he feared for his life. The guerrillas had approached him in Puerto Sábalo to demand a 10 per cent levy on the income from the community's new carbon-bond scheme. Manuel had refused, he said, and the night before he had been cornered by a guerrilla known as *El Paisa*, who had given him a few hours to leave Puerto Sábalo. Manuel said he needed to get out of the jungle as soon as possible, and insisted that Castro help his family do the same. By chance, a military aircraft had arrived that same day, and Castro persuaded the pilot to take Manuel to San José del Guaviare.

Now, Magdalena stood before Castro's desk in the same place that her boyfriend had been a week earlier. Her request for safe passage out of the jungle was complicated by the fact that there were no military flights scheduled for the coming weeks. The next day, however, the weekly cargo flight would set off to San José del Guaviare. Castro had no authority to force the pilot to take the family, so the best he could do would be to appeal to the pilot's sense of humanitarian duty.

Magdalena seemed content with this solution. She had relatives in Araracuara who could put her family up for the night. While they waited for the plane, she reasoned that it would be a good time to have Cristin vaccinated in the small clinic at Puerto Santander, on the other side of the river.

That afternoon, she led her family down the road that descended on the other side of the tupui into Araracuara. The town was laid out in an Indigenous mold. The one-story wooden houses were spaced apart: some sitting in fields; others, nestled in the forest, and linked by footpaths. In the center, its cloister of dormitories and classrooms surrounded by fruit trees, was the village's most prominent public building, the Internado, the Catholic boarding school where Magdalena had studied many years earlier.

As they walked the path that led by the riverside, Tien lagged behind, transfixed by the fishermen. On the large boulders that dotted the river, there were cantilevered platforms made from thick bamboo that jutted out over the water. The men stood motionless, arms cocked, harpoon in hand, waiting to spot a giant catfish. Lesly hurried Tien along, ushering him towards the grassy bank where their mother was hailing a boatman to cross the river.

On the other side lay Puerto Santander. It was inhabited by

colonos, white settlers who had moved to the jungle in the second half of the twentieth century. Its streets were laid out in a grid pattern with breezeblock houses several stories high that backed onto one another. Up the hill was a modest medical center, where a solitary junior doctor provided basic treatment for the surrounding population.

Magdalena boarded the children, and the lancha began its slow passage across the river. Twenty years earlier, Magdalena had made the same journey when she escaped Araracuara for the first time.

CHAPTER THREE

Black Sheep

A month later, when her body was identified in the wreckage of the Cessna 206, a single photograph of Magdalena Mucutuy circulated in the local media. It showed her in half-profile against a wooden-paneled wall, wearing a red blouse with white trim, her hair tied back from her face. Her expression was serious and attentive, as if she were listening to a speech in the maloca. She looked small and demure. She looked, to many Colombians, like their idea of a typical Indigenous woman.

In the subsequent drama of the search for her missing children, Magdalena's role in events was largely overlooked. She remained a hole at the center of the story. But her life, her character, and the tough decisions she had to confront created the circumstances that led her and her family to board the Cessna in May 2023. They were indicative, too, of the precarious position of many women across the Amazon.

In the jungle's Indigenous communities, gender roles remain strictly defined. Men are expected to learn to hunt, build, or trade, and to assume positions of leadership in the community. In the malocas, the decisions are usually made in male-only areas, often under the influence of sacred recipes such as mambé, prohibited to women. Girls receive schooling, but, for many, their real education is considered to be the acquisition of skills needed to make a good wife: growing and cooking food, doing domestic chores, raising children.

Since the 1980s, wealthy Colombians in the cities have preferred to hire Indigenous maids, believing them to be obedient and hardworking, prepared to accept a meager salary without fuss. And while that image has shifted somewhat as Indigenous women have gained prominence in Colombian public life, Magdalena, growing up in the 1990s, seemed to conform to stereotype.

Today, when asked to describe her daughter, Fatima Mucuty's first instinct is to praise her industriousness. "You never had to tell her what to do—she was always working," she says. "If there were clothes to be washed or the porch was dirty, she wasn't the sort who frowns. She just got on with it, always laughing."

Manuel, explaining what first attracted him to Magdalena, says, "She was very capable, very hardworking. She took good care of my clothes, she cooked well, and she looked after me."

But her childhood friend Diana Rodriguez remembers a different side of Magdalena, a girl with an exuberant love of sport, a curiosity about the world, and an impulsive and defiant streak.

In a Bogotá café, on a typically cold and wet afternoon, Diana hunches protectively over her cup. Today, she is one of an estimated 20,000 Indigenous to have left their home territories and relocated to Bogotá since 1990. She is thirty-five years old and wrapped in a thick down jacket, her hair pulled sternly back from a square face. On her right temple is a large C-shaped scar, dealt to her by a guerrilla's rifle butt when she was eleven. She looks tough, but when she talks of Magdalena and their childhood beside the Caquetá, her face softens.

The best times were the afternoons they spent rocking in a canoe. If they felt like fishing, they could pull up a hearty catch with a simple hook and line. Other times, they would dare each other to paddle up close to the rapids, laughing as the canoe keeled and spun, grabbing at branches or rocks to prevent it turning over. If they got word of a capsized trading boat upstream, they would scavenge for washed-up merchandise. They amassed a collection of flip-flops in different colors and sizes.

They studied at the Internado, the school in Araracuara founded and run by Capuchin monks. Diana was a day pupil; Magdalena, a boarder. In the mornings they studied, and in the afternoons they sang in the choir and played sports on the school's concrete field. Diana excelled in basketball; Magdalena preferred five-a-side soccer.

In September 2004, practice took a serious turn. Magdalena and Diana would wake at dawn to attend training with the older girls and women of the community. For the first time, Araracuara was fielding a squad to compete in a sports tournament the paisanos dubbed "the Indigenous Olympics." Although its youngest member, Magdalena's skillful play made her a vital member of the soccer team, and she didn't want to let her teammates down.

The problem was that the tournament was to be held in La Chorrera, an Indigenous town sixty kilometers to the south, close to the border with Peru. It could only be reached by undertaking a five-day trek through the jungle, and Fatima and Narciso, Magdalena's parents, would hear nothing of it. As far as they were concerned, the trip was far too dangerous for a fourteen-year-old girl.

In the first light of one November morning, Diana waited by the waterside, unsure if her friend would come. Downstream from where the fishermen stalked their catfish, on the calmer stretch in front of Puerto Santander, the boulders were smaller and rounded, half-submerged in the water. Their surfaces were wrinkly with petroglyphs—smiling faces, spirals, serpents— painstakingly carved by an ancient people. Diana was sitting on these rocks when she saw Magdalena emerge through the trees.

"She came running down the path, she was flying," remembers Diana. The two girls boarded a lancha, and pressed some crumpled peso bills into the boatman's hand.

"Let's go, let's get out of here right now," said Magdalena.

When they reached Puerto Santander, they hid in the grounds of the church. Magdalena was worried that a family member might spot her and stop her from making the trip. But soon, as they peered over the church wall, they spotted the rest of the Araracuara sporting delegation arrive at the riverside and begin their march uphill towards the trail head. Gathering their things, Diana and Magdalena rushed to catch up with their companions.

"When we were in the middle of the group and into the forest, Magdalena calmed down, she started to laugh," says Diana. "She said, 'When I go back, do you think my mom will punish me?' She wasn't worried about leaving—she was worried about returning."

But Magdalena wouldn't have to face Fatima's ire. She wouldn't see her mother again for ten years.

The 2004 trip to La Chorrera was also the last time that Diana and Magdalena were together. The following year, Diana was offered a job purportedly working on one of the trading boats that worked the Caquetá River. It was a trap. She was taken instead to a jungle camp to be enrolled in the FARC. She managed to escape, and in 2008 she moved to Bogotá as a *desplazada*, a displaced person. Since then, life in the city had been tough.

"I wanted to leave the jungle. I knew how to cook, how to clean, and I kidded myself that life in the city would be easier," she says. "It turns out, it's more difficult."

Diana never had a chance to say goodbye to Magdalena. She had always assumed that they would meet again; even after she left the jungle, Diana's gut told her that one day Magdelana would show up in Bogotá. She had always detected a restlessness in her friend, a desire to escape the jungle and the humdrum life of chores and housework that she felt had been planned for her. Diana recalls that, often, when the two of them were sitting in the canoe, Magdalena would look sadly at the trading boats as they passed them, headed downstream. Then she would turn to Diana and say: "Wouldn't it be great if it stopped to pick us up, if they took us away from here?"

The trail from Araracuara to La Chorrera was every bit as treacherous as Magdalena's parents had warned. From the air, the jungle appears as flat as a green ocean, but it's an illusion created by the trees growing to the same height. Beneath the canopy, Magdalena and Diana climbed steep, muddy hills, and descended into valleys where the path disappeared into streams and the water came up to their chests.

They ate tinned sardines and casabe, and, on one occasion, a monkey stew proudly prepared by one of the hunting parties. In the evenings, they applied salt to their chafed thighs and gossiped in their hammocks. Magdalena peppered Diana with questions about her new boyfriend, a corporal in the navy, who had given her clothes and food before they set off. Magdalena was curious, perhaps a little envious. She had not yet had a boyfriend.

During the day, Magdalena impressed her teammates with her ability to identify food in the jungle.

"She was one of those people who would be walking along

and then suddenly start pulling at a tree," says Diana. She would come back chewing on a fruit or a seed, and offer it around to her companions. But as she strayed into the undergrowth, Magdalena noticed that some of the tree trunks bore faded scars.

The path they walked on was an artifact of a holocaust. It had been hacked through the jungle in the first years of the twentieth century by Indigenous labor. For two decades, it had been trodden by thousands of Uitoto, Andoque, and Muinane people bearing heavy loads of cured latex. Across the wider Amazon region, the rise of the rubber industry to meet global demand for pneumatic tires had devastating effects on Indigenous tribes. None paid a higher price than the People of the Center. In the Caquetá-Putumayo basin, the latex-bearing *siringa* trees were of a lesser quality than those in Peru and Brazil, and the rapids and waterfalls on the basin's rivers made transportation costs exorbitant. What the region did possess was a large potential workforce that had had little prior contact with the market economy. Julio Cesár Arana, a Peruvian straw-hat salesman turned riverboat magnate, was determined to squeeze the population for every last drop of profit.

Backed by British capital, his Peruvian Rubber Company established dozens of plantations where a white "captain" was assisted by a small cadre of black laborers from Barbados. The heavy work of enslaving entire tribes was delegated to the Indigenous themselves. Local young men, known as *muchachos*, were given rifles, trained in brutality, and sent out to hunt their rivals. Those captured, or "civilized," in the company's terminology, were subjected to back-breaking labor. Mornings were spent bleeding the siringa trees and collecting their sap. In the afternoons, they hammered the latex and cured it in earth ovens for transportation to ports.

The impact of the rubber industry on the People of the Center was devastating. At the turn of the century, their population was estimated at between 50,000 and 100,000. Two decades later, fewer than 10,000 would remain. The stories of the sadistic punishments carried out by the rubber barons eventually found their way into the Western press. They published reports of thousands of Indigenous lashed to death, of women raped in front of their husbands, of limbs cut off for punishment or entertainment, and of babies' heads dashed against tree trunks. In language quite new to the time, the British consul sent to investigate the Peruvian Rubber Company described its actions as a "crime against humanity."

But Magdalena, like many of her generation, had learned little about this dark period in her people's history. There were still Uitoto elders who remembered the stories their grandparents had told them. They could identify the spots on the jungle path where their ancestors had been executed. They knew where the ruins of the malocas, burned down with entire clans inside, were located in the distant heart of the monte. They could tell you which clans had resisted the whites and which had collaborated. But they had vowed not to pass on this dangerous knowledge.

In the years after the rubber boom, the People of the Center had tried to rebuild their shattered world. They abandoned their old homes in the depths of the monte, and built new communities, such as Puerto Sábalo, on the banks of the rivers. The memories of the rubber boom, along with earlier histories of clan conflict and witchcraft, were buried by the elders in a symbolic *basket of darkness*. This basket could never be opened; it represented the "nuclear arsenal" of memory that could only lead to war.

When Magdalena, Diana, and the rest of the Araracuara delegation reached the end of the old rubber trail, they marched along a mud road until they came to a grand building the like of which the girls had never seen before. It had thick stone walls with wide wooden balconies on the upper floor. The "Casa Arana," as it was known, had been the headquarters of the Peruvian Rubber Company. Now it was a school. The breezy upper floors, with their views over the treetops, once the living quarters of the white employees, had been converted into dormitories for students. Below, the dungeons that had once held Uitoto prisoners were now storage rooms for desks and chairs. The Casa Arana had become a symbol of the endurance of Indigenous culture against the ravages of extractive capitalism. The People of the Center chose to look to the future rather than the past.

In order to survive what remained of the twentieth century and to rebuild their former way of life, the tribes' caciques opened up what they called *the basket of life*. It contained all the ancient knowledge that their ancestors had accumulated about life and fecundity. It included agricultural techniques, advice for raising children, and recipes and rituals. The People of the Center, in common with other Amazonian peoples, view the territory as a living being, where one's actions in the immediate surroundings have consequences in the wider environment.

Anthropologists have often marveled at their understanding of the symbiotic relationships between different species of plants and the complex jungle gardens, interspersed with fruit trees, that they plant. In the wake of the holocaust, old divisions between tribes and clans were set aside. The philosophy that united them, one that prioritized "abundance"—of food, children, life in general—was used to strengthen cooperation between the groups. Intermarriage between tribes became the norm and, in the 1970s, the first Indigenous political organizations were established. In 1988, in an attempt to turn the page on this shameful episode, Colombian president Virgilio Barco, sporting a feathered headdress, chose the steps of the Casa Arana to announce the return of six million hectares of Amazonian land to Indigenous ownership.

In November 2004, the Casa Arana, still eerily resistant to the rot and erosion of the jungle, hosted the opening ceremony of the Indigenous Olympics. Sport, too, could be a powerful promoter of inter-tribe cooperation and solidarity. Diana and Magdalena were delighted to mingle with Indigenous athletes and supporters from the Amazon and beyond. When it was discovered that one of the Araracuara team was still somewhere back on the trail, Magdalena, the youngest and the fittest, was thrust into running the long-distance race. Diana remembers her running in bare feet, maintaining a steady pace, and overtaking the early leaders in the final stretch.

"Everyone was laughing, they couldn't believe it," she recalls. "How can she run barefoot after almost a week walking in the jungle? They thought her feet must be covered in blisters."

On the sidelines, a twenty-two-year-old local Uitoto man nudged his friend.

"Who's the girl from Araracuara?" he asked.

Andrés Jacobombaire was the son of the governor of Santa Maria, one of the twenty-two communities that formed La Chorrera. He had spiky black hair, and wore clothes muddied from an afternoon spent playing in goal for his soccer team. The next day, as Magdalena and her teammates sought the shade at half-time in their match, he walked over and offered her a cup of tinto, the local sweet, dark coffee. He told her she played like Carlos Valderrama, the blond-permed idol of the Colombian national team.

"It was love at first sight," remembers Andrés. "She was pretty, but also she was *del ambiente*." By which he means she was social, engaging, fun to be around. The following evening, at the closing-night party in an old wooden warehouse that doubled as a bar, he asked Magdalena onto the sweaty dance floor. They danced hand-in-hand to salsa, held each other close for the Vallenato's melancholy accordions, and, finally, swayed together for a merengue, Magdalena's favorite. They kissed. They said goodbye.

The next morning, the Araracuara team prepared to leave La Chorrera. The team manager had settled on a good price with a boatman, who had agreed to take them further upriver, cutting the return trek to just two days. But on the lancha, Diana detected a change in Magdalena. Throughout the tournament, she had been cheerful and gregarious, excited to be in a new place, with new people. Now, she sat with her head bowed, staring into the depths of the water.

When they disembarked later that afternoon and began the trek back to Araracuara, Magdalena seemed to dawdle, lost in thought. Diana kept her company, but soon she realized that they had fallen far behind the rest of the party. Somewhere up ahead a gunshot sounded. The hunting party had spotted a monkey, she supposed. It seemed to bring Magdalena out of her trance.

"You go on," Magdalen told her friend. "I'm going to stay. I'm going back to La Chorrera."

She turned on her heels and began running back the way they had come. Diana chased after her. When they reached the banks of the river, the boatman had already departed, but he heard their yells and turned around to pick them up. They had gotten lost,

Magdalena explained to him. It was a white lie that she repeated to concerned paisanos when they arrived back in La Chorrera.

For two nights, they slept in Andrés' parents' house, a typical two-room build with its wooden slats smartly painted in red and brown. As they sat on the porch overlooking a small soccer pitch opposite, Magdalena told Diana that she would not return to Araracuara. She knew she'd be punished for defying her parents, but that wasn't what concerned her. She didn't want to return to the life of chores, and she didn't want to live her whole life on the Caquetá River. Besides, Andrés was good-looking and kind. Maybe it would work out.

The next day, Diana was offered a free seat in a cargo flight back to Araracuara by a pilot who knew her mother. Magdalena would live the next thirteen years of her life in La Chorrera.

Today, the inhabitants of the town have warm memories of the young runaway. They pulled together to help her. When Andrés' parents made it clear that they could not have an unmarried couple living under their roof, Magdalena was taken in by Ermalita Rotieroke, a single mother of three who lived nearby. She offered Magdalena food and lodging in return for help with the housework and childcare.

The girl from Chukiki quickly became part of the family. Ermalita helped her enroll in a local school, where she could complete her final year of education. When Magdalena took her first communion, Ermalita's brother and sister-in-law stepped in as godparents.

"She was a good girl," Adelia Rotieroke, Magdalena's godmother, told me in La Chorrera. "With Ermalita, she was often out growing manioc. They used to make delicious stews together. She loved to play soccer and make handicrafts. She was always happy, I can still remember her smile and how she used to tease her godfather, calling him grumpy, trying to get him to laugh."

With no family or friends in her new home, Magdalena was in a precarious position. Neighbors recall that it was she who pursued Andrés in the coming weeks. He had been worried that she was too young, but she soon won him over.

On one occasion, early in their relationship, Andrés took Magdalena to see the bridge that crossed a run of white-water rapids on the edge of town. It was a suspension bridge, fifty meters long, a shaky collaboration of planks, wooden handrails, and steel cables. Magdalena had never seen anything like it. She was terrified by the way it swayed, by the sight of the frothing water through the gaps in the slats, Andrés recalls, but he told her to hold the handrail, and she made it to the center of the bridge, where she took in the view.

"It's beautiful," she said.

La Chorrera sits in one of the most picturesque settings in the Amazon jungle. The rapids beneath the bridge enter into a wide backwater in which two large sandbanks—one golden and one blueish-gray in color—protrude like islands in a tropical lagoon. All around, the forest rises on gentle, low hills. Wooden houses, their terraces angled towards the water, poke through the foliage. On the far bank from the bridge, the wide gable roof and long wooden balconies of the Casa Arana can be seen above the palms.

In the months that followed, Magdalena came to love La Chorrera. Compared to Araracuara, there was far more to do, more shops, restaurants, and places to socialize. The town was growing rapidly as paisanos built their communities along the jungle paths and waterways that radiated from the town. In total, there were twenty-two communities, and they mingled freely. And it was safer. The grip of the "left hand" was weaker, the paisanos were friendly and outgoing, and you didn't have to watch what you said.

Above all, Magdalena loved the traditional dances held in the malocas. These ceremonies, which had seemed at risk of dying out following the rubber boom, were resurgent in La Chorrera. Magdalena and her girlfriends would paint their arms and faces with the dark ink of the Kipara fruit and hold hands, gliding back and forth as the men swung palm fronds overhead.

It was after one such dance, in late 2006, that Andrés invited her to live with him in a maloca that his family owned eight kilometers out of town, along the path to Araracuara and next to an expansive chagra.

In August 2007, their first child, Angie, was born, and the following year the couple were married in a small white church on the hill overlooking La Chorrera. It was a Catholic ceremony, but afterwards the couple went to celebrate in the traditional way in the maloca on the outskirts of town. The locals approved of the match.

"It was a good wedding, they put on a lot of food," says Adelia. "We always liked Magdalena, and she had found a good husband, one that didn't drink or hit her. They had food, and they could look after their children."

Andrés keeps a photo of that day on his phone. It shows Magdalena dressed in a white dress and elbow-high gloves, holding a tiny bouquet of red flowers. On her left is Andrés, decked out in black pants and a white shirt that billows around his arms. Between them, holding both their hands, is Angie, a toddler in a green dress. Magdalena sent a copy of this photo to her mother, Fatima.

The newlyweds lived a simple life. Magdalena tended the chagra while Andrés worked as a logger, felling forest with a chainsaw to open up new cultivation areas and earning extra pesos selling planks and slats as construction materials. His prized possession was his rifle, with which he would hunt in the monte, bringing back game, usually wild turkeys or monkey, for Magdalena to cook up.

On weekends, they would come into town to visit Andrés' parents. His father regaled Magdalena with the clan's oral history, and taught her the local songs. From her mother-in-law she learned new recipes such as for *tucupí*, the local spicy sauce made from manioc juice. Over time, Andrés would build them a new house in the grounds behind, with two bedrooms set on high stilts, but for now they continued to live out of town, close to their crops. Uitoto tradition has it that children conceived on the chagra will grow up to be strong and resourceful. Lesly was born in November 2009, and then a boy, John Andrés, and a girl, Soleiny, followed.

"They lived well, they often came to visit us," says one neighbor. "We had a lot of celebrations here, everyone was happy. But when her mother came, everything changed."

I first meet Fatima Mucutuy in a restaurant in Villavicencio, a city at the foot of the Andes. She is in her late sixties with a thin, slight body, and her right eye is a cloudy gray. Before our conversation starts, she unscrews a small tub of ambil, and applies the paste to her tongue. If her appearance suggests fragility, the impression quickly disappears when she speaks. Fatima is assertive and outspoken, and she's been that way, she insists, all her life.

"I was born this way," she says. "My father and my husband told me not to talk so loud, not to laugh so much, but I can't live being bitter. I live at the rhythm of the monte."

The monte, the untamed jungle beyond the settlements, had always held a fascination for Fatima. As a young woman, she was something of a free spirit, spending time on the Brazilian side of the border, where she grew her knowledge of jungle plants and different Indigenous cultures. In Magdalena she had an eager student. "She really liked working on the chagra—she loved to grow pineapples, she loved to sow," she says. "Whatever fruit you liked, she'd say, 'Watch, I'll sow it.' She wouldn't let people throw away the seeds." In November 2004, that education came to an abrupt end. "We never gave her permission to go to La Chorrera," she says. "She was only fourteen, it was very irresponsible."

By Christmas 2014, Fatima had not seen her daughter in ten years. None of Magdalena's family had been able to attend her wedding. Money was too tight to afford a place on one of the cargo flights to La Chorrera, and, with her own young children to look after, the five-day trek was out of the question. Fatima was also tortured by the impression that her daughter had made a poor marriage decision. Andrés may have been the son of a Uitoto *mayor*, but the Jacobombaire name was not one that resonated with people in Araracuara. To add insult to injury, Andrés had not made the trip to Chukiki to ask Narciso for Magdalena's hand in marriage.

The photo of the wedding that Magdalena sent seemed to Fatima to confirm her suspicions. Taken in the maloca, where the backlighting blurred her expression slightly, Magdalena's face wore a grimace rather than a smile

In the years since her departure, Fatima had spoken regularly with Magdalena on the phone, but now the calls had become less frequent. She always had the nagging feeling that her daughter wasn't telling her everything, that her living conditions were not as comfortable as she made out. "I was very anguished," says

Fatima. "I always missed her, but she had started to forget about me, and I suffered a lot in those years that I didn't see her." In December 2014, accompanied by three of her adult children and a grandchild, Fatima set off on the trek to La Chorrera to see her daughter.

It says something of Fatima's personality and charisma that the population of Santa Maria still recall her visit vividly after almost a decade. She made her presence felt. By day, she made her rounds of the town's pregnant and ailing population, employing her skills as a midwife and traditional healer. By night, she took Magdalena out to the local bars. The visit, however, did nothing to convince her that her daughter was living well. The house that Andrés had built behind his parents' house lacked charm. To her eyes, Magdalena seemed skinny and poorly turned out. "Everything was run down, she didn't have good clothes," she said. "It broke my heart, but I didn't say anything. I told her to brush her hair, because she looked like an old lady." She gave her daughter some new clothes and a health check-up.

The chagra, by comparison, was organized and clean. Fatima was impressed by its yams, plantains, and excellent manioc. Her daughter had lost none of her work ethic. In the two weeks she stayed, Fatima saw her constantly cleaning, sweeping, and cooking, never letting anyone else raise a finger. Fatima detected an overbearing and bossy mother-in-law who allowed her son to laze around and never stuck up for his wife. With a touch of small-town envy, she felt that if Magdalena had moved to La Chorrera to better herself, in reality her situation was worse than it would have been closer to her mother in Chukiki. "I only said a few words," recalls Fatima. "I said, 'Daughter, you're working like a donkey and your husband won't even go hunting, even though he has a rifle.'"

The residents of Santa Maria remember it as more than a few words. In their view, Fatima's criticisms were loud and frequent. It seemed, they said, that she was determined to separate the couple. When Fatima left after her two-week stay, they began to hear raised voices emanating from the small house on stilts for the first time they could remember. Andrés' mother told anyone who would listen that Magdalena was parroting Fatima's complaints, using the very same words. They were poor, he was lazy, he wasn't a good husband or father. In early 2015, Angie fell sick, and Andrés took her to Leticia for treatment for several days. According to Fatima, Magdalena was convinced he was having an affair.

In the months that followed, Andrés tried to smooth things over. In November 2015, accompanied by Magdalena, Lesly, and Soleiny, he made the trip to Chukiki. They were warmly received; Narciso was *buena gente*, a good guy, and forgave him for not having asked for Magdalena's hand. They fished together, and shared ambil and mambé. Andrés worked tirelessly on the chagra, cutting back the trees with his chainsaw, burning the trunks. But towards the end of his stay, Andrés came down with yellow fever, which left him shivering and sweating. He recovered enough to make the return trip to La Chorrera, but when he arrived, his friends and family noted that his speech had slowed—the words seemed to stall on the tip of his tongue.

Worse was to follow. One afternoon in February 2017, Andrés was in La Chorrera, working on the chagra with Magdalena. At one side of the plot, he had constructed a platform of planks, two meters off the ground, from which he was trimming back the branches of the trees. He was approaching the end of his day's work, looking up at the next tree, when he stepped backwards into a gap between two sections of the platform. He fell backwards, throwing the whirring chainsaw to one side, but landing on a tree stump below, his spine taking the full impact. His first thought was that he had broken his back. Magdalena rushed to get the help of a neighbor, and together they helped Andrés stumble back to the maloca. There he rested, but he never recovered. Just as his speech left him gradually, he began to lose movement in his legs. The local medical center was unequipped to provide him with anything more than rudimentary treatment. In the months that followed, Andrés' condition would deteriorate to the point where his movement was reduced to slow, tiny steps.

Although largely incapacitated, Andrés had lost none of his mental faculties, and his neighbors felt he could still contribute to the community. Later that year, he was made governor of Santa Maria, which required him to attend meetings in a maloca in the center of La Chorrera. One day in September 2017, he returned home at five in the afternoon to find Angie, his eldest, running towards him. She told him that her mother had taken Lesly, then aged seven, and Soleiny, a babe in arms, on the flight to Araracuara. He remembered an argument he had had with his wife that morning—a stupid argument about a package of clothes and kitchenware that she wanted to send to her mother. That evening, one of his neighbors told him that he had been at the airstrip and had seen Magdalena deliver a package to the woman who weighed the cargo on a springed hook. At the last moment, he said, she had taken her daughters by the hand and boarded the plane.

That afternoon in Araracuara, Fatima had waited by the airstrip for Magdalena's package. That her daughter and two granddaughters would be on the flight as well had never crossed her mind. "I never thought my daughter would come," she says.

"Everyone was happy. The people around said, 'Magda, how long has it been since we saw you last?'"

Today in La Chorrera, the family and neighbors in Santa Maria are still saddened by Magdalena's departure. They say that Andrés was a good husband who provided for his wife as best he could until he was struck by illness and injury. "Magdalena told me, 'I can't take it anymore—he doesn't work, he doesn't do anything,'" recalls one of her neighbors. "I told her, 'That's because he's sick. You know that when he was healthy, he worked, he shared with you.' But she said, 'That doesn't help me anymore.'" That she took two of his children to live by the Caquetá River, eventually under the roof of another man, is considered an act of negligence. Such scenarios are repeated across Colombia, and the emotions that follow often run highest and the fallout is most widespread in small communities. Not for nothing is there a local expression *"Pueblo pequeño, infierno grande"*—"Small town, big hell." In the Colombian Amazon, these feelings are accentuated by poverty and remoteness.

Andrés says he called Magdalena repeatedly, trying to convince her to return for the good of Angie and John Andrés, the two children she had left behind. But, he recalls, Magdalena was cold to his protests. "Look, Andrés, it's over," she told him, before hanging up.

When Andrés talks about this moment, his voice cracks with sadness and a hint of anger. He wonders if he had failed to read the signs. He had always detected a melancholy side to Magdalena, had sensed that she was holding a secret. One day, early in their relationship, he had noticed a deep scar on her right calf. When pressed, she told him that it was the result of a beating she had received. She said her childhood had not been a happy one, that she received less affection than her siblings, and that she had been obliged to undertake the most chores. Andrés deduced that this is what led her to seek a new life in La Chorrera. "I'm the black sheep of the family," she had told him.

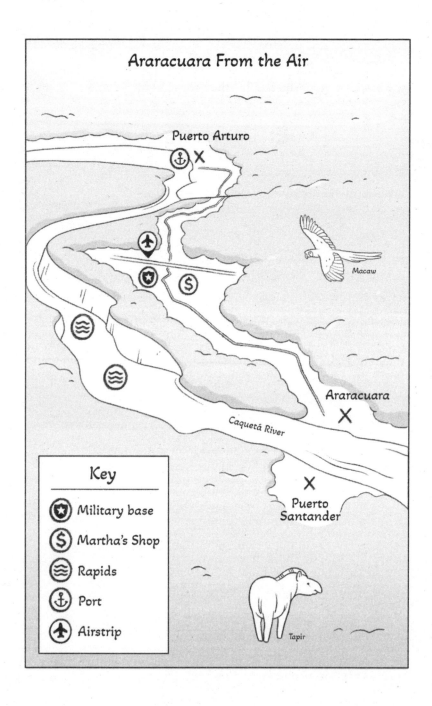

CHAPTER FOUR

El Carramán

In his 1967 novel, *One Hundred Years of Solitude*, Colombian author Gabriel García Márquez introduced the world to the fictional town of Macondo. It was presented as an Eden of innocence set by a river that ran over a bed of huge white stones "like prehistoric eggs." The inhabitants took the supernatural in their stride. Children were born with pigs' tails, priests levitated at the altar, lovers walked in clouds of yellow butterflies. All of this, to them, seemed everyday. The products of the modern age, however, struck them with awe and fear. Over the course of the novel's pages, a series of outsiders brought them into contact with ice-makers, railroads, and the machine gun. The results were rarely short of disastrous for the community.

Garcia Márquez took inspiration for many of his characters from his childhood spent in a sleepy village near Colombia's Caribbean coast. However, to do justice to the isolation of the novel's title, he set Macondo in the depths of the jungle. There, presumably, the contrast between the past and the present, between innocence and cynicism, would be most stark. Araracuara is a town in the Macondian mold.

The settlement takes its name from an Indigenous word meaning "macaw's nest." The tupui that overlooks the town is split through the middle by a thundering, livid stretch of the Caquetá River. On the cliffs that face each other, fifty meters apart, scores of blue and yellow macaws make their homes in narrow cracks and ledges. In the twilight hours, they emerge squawking from the shade to soar though the gorge. Viewed from the lip of the chasm, at a point that the paisanos call "Devil's Leap," it's a beautiful, primordial scene. The scattered beer cans in the undergrowth testify to the viewpoint's popularity with local friends and lovers.

The rapids below are impassable by boat. While the Amazon River and its more placid tributaries were well navigated by Portuguese traders in the sixteenth and seventeenth centuries, this turbulent funnel of white water marked the end of the line for all but the hardiest explorers. Even today, those coming downriver, as Magdalena and her family had, must disembark at Puerto Arturo, climb to the crest of the tupui, and descend to where the waters discharged by the gorge settle into the wider, calmer stretch of river, by the banks of the town.

The tupui, therefore, has a strategic importance. On the opposite side of the gorge, several clandestine jungle trails allow traffickers to move coca leaf or marijuana around the gorge, but all regular cargo and passengers must transit past the airstrip and the army base that sit on the summit of the tupui.

Long before the military settled on this point as a base from which to launch assaults on the guerrilla forces in the jungle, Araracuara had been the center of a more ambitious plan. From 1938 to 1971, the town had been a penal colony, an open-air prison where thousands of common criminals were sent for hard labor.

In the 1930s, Colombia had fought a war with Peru for control of the Caquetá-Putumayo basin. Afterwards, the politicians decided that the only way to maintain control of the distant southern border was to establish a white settlement with a functioning economy. Araracuara was to become the "Colombian Australia." Over the course of the colony's existence, 2,800 convicts found themselves clearing forests, cultivating crops, and raising cattle.

There was no need for barbed wire. The sheer isolation, the inhospitable jungle, and the treacherous river rapids were enough to discourage flight. The only man known to have escaped the colony did so by hugging the landing gear of a cargo plane. When it touched down in Bogotá four hours later, the half-frozen fugitive was promptly rearrested.

But the same conditions that made escape impossible made settlement undesirable. The project's "civilizing mission" failed. When it was finally wrapped up, a few colonists settled in Puerto Santander, but a sustainable economy never took root. The prison's offices and warehouses in Araracuara fell into ruin, and the cattle ranches were quickly reabsorbed into the jungle.

It left a lasting impact on the Indigenous population, however. Uitoto and Muinane men were pressed into low-paying jobs with the colony as guards or boatmen. Growing up in the shadow of the colony, Fatima remembers that girls and women were on guard against a constant threat of sexual assault from the prisoners. The attempt to build a market economy led to over-fishing and over-hunting for sale to the colony, and left behind an appetite for alcohol among the paisanos that has remained a problem ever since.

The airstrip that the prisoners built and the road that linked to it were the last functioning inheritance of the colony. In the 1990s, it was still smoothly paved in the service of a radar base that had been installed at the end of the runway by the US Drug Enforcement Administration. Until 1996 an OV-10 Bronco, a light attack aircraft with distinctive twin booms, stood ready to scramble and shoot down suspected drug flights.

When Magdalena and her family trudged across it in April 2023, only the occasional thin sliver of tarmac at its fringes hinted at the airstrip's former glory. Now, it was little more than a long carpet of gravel spread out over the rock face. Funds to repave it had been petitioned often but delivered only once, and that time they had been embezzled by negotiators.

Although longer than many other jungle airstrips, the gravel runway was hazardous. In 2014, a two-engine Piper had crashed shortly after takeoff from Araracuara, killing all eight passengers. Today, opposite the army base, the fuselage of a C-46 air taxi that crash-landed in the 1960s shines like a mirror, its paintwork stripped away by fifty years of sun, a visual reminder of the airstrip's perils.

One hundred meters from where the road leaves the airstrip and descends towards Araracuara is a shop. It has white painted walls and a thick wooden window that folds down to become a countertop. An extended corrugated-iron roof provides a shaded porch for the benches of an outdoor patio. Around it, a white picket fence hints at the owner's pride in her little parcel of the jungle.

Martha Muñoz arrived in Araracuara in the mid-1980s as the nineteen-year-old wife of a postal clerk. Her husband was assuming a post that had lain vacant for months after its previous occupant contracted malaria. For a decade, they lived in the town, in a house belonging to the national telecoms company, which had a tall antenna in the backyard. In 1999, the FARC guerrillas arrived. They toppled the antenna and made off with the solar panels that powered it. The flights that brought in mail were canceled, and Martha's husband found himself out of the job.

"They took everything, and left us without any means of communication," she says. "But we'd put roots down here, so we stayed and set up as traders."

Almost thirty years later, Martha's shop is the hub of social and commercial life in Araracuara. From morning until dusk, the shaded patio is a place where paisanos, soldiers, and visitors from Bogotá come to buy produce or use the wifi provided by the small satellite dish on the roof.

When I visited the shop in November 2023, Martha was busy serving customers, placing phone calls, and greeting passers-by. She wore a loose-fitting terracotta T-shirt, light make-up, and a pair of earrings. On her head was a pair of pink spectacles that she occasionally flipped down to her nose to read an incoming text. I watched as she performed an array of roles with an unfussy and decisive manner honed on the frontier. In the Colombian Amazon, ordinary people often assume extraordinary responsibilities.

In addition to selling food and internet connections, Martha dispatches, stores, and delivers packages from the weekly cargo flights. In a town with no other financial services, she is its banker, transferring money on her phone, and taking in and paying out cash from the till. At the back of the shop, she rents a spare room to passengers with an early-morning flight. She is also the closest thing the airstrip has to a control tower. Over WhatsApp, she sends photos of the runway and the weather conditions to incoming pilots.

"This is a strategic position, and I try to help out everyone who comes through here," she says when the flow of customers finally abates. "I always try to repay a favor, and I've come to know everyone in the town."

Tuesday mornings were always busy. The weekly cargo from San José del Guaviare was delivered by a twin-engine Antanov 26, which arrived around 9.00 am and took off an hour later. From the early hours, Martha was busy matching passengers with seats on the outgoing plane, feeding and hydrating travelers, receiving and dispatching cargo. On April 17, half an hour after she heard the roar of the Antanov's engines as it took off from the airstrip, she saw Magdalena Mucutuy approach the counter with a baby in her arms.

Martha was fond of Magdalena, and she was delighted to see how much Cristin had grown. Nine months before, she'd seen her as a newborn when Manuel had brought her into town to register her birth. Now she was strong and restless, wrestling to escape her mother's grip and crawl across the counter.

Magdalena explained that she hadn't been able to board the cargo flight. Superintendent Castro had tried to convince the pilot to take the family for free, but the pilot had refused. They would have to wait a week until the next flight. In the meantime, they could stay in her great-uncle's house, but Magdalena asked Martha if she could hold onto a bag of clothes and a file containing the children's documents.

In return, Martha handed her a letter that Manuel had left for her the previous week. As she watched her read its contents, Martha felt sad that another young Uitoto family was leaving the territory for good.

"That day, I said to her, 'Why don't you stay? The carbon-bonds thing is just starting up, and it will bring money. Your family will help you in the meantime,'" she recalls.

But Magdalena was adamant. She told Martha that she had exhausted the hospitality of her family and friends. She saw no future in the jungle.

"Manuel is the only one who will look after me and the children," she told Martha.

"Her mind was made up," recalls Martha. "She was going to live with Carramán."

Manuel Ranoque says he doesn't know why they called him *Carramán*—just that he'd been given the nickname as a teenager, and it had followed him around ever since. Even the paisanos couldn't agree on its meaning. Some said the word meant a tearaway, perhaps a bum, and came from his scruffy appearance, his fondness for marijuana, and his habit of walking around barefoot. Others said it described a person of imposing physique and character.

Manuel was the kind of man to earn a sticky nickname. From an early age, he'd set out to make an impression on his world, and he'd been rewarded with notoriety.

He was born in Puerto Sábalo in 1992. His mother was the daughter of a cacique and married to a Uitoto man. But Manuel's dark complexion, his muscular frame, and his tightly curled hair led many in the village to speculate that his father was a different man, possibly an Afro-Colombian former inmate of the prison colony. Some of the elders of Puerto Sábalo remember Manuel as a *gamín*, an urchin or troublemaker, but his own recollection of his childhood is different. He chooses to remember the evenings spent in the maloca with his grandfather, singing Uitoto songs, and learning the medicinal and spiritual application of the forest plants.

"My grandparents came from the monte," he says. "I was very close to my grandfather. He understood that, even as a boy, I was fascinated by the native language. He had trained to be a shaman, and I wanted to be like him, to take ambil and dish out caguana [a traditional pineapple juice], to build a maloca. I wanted to learn the words of life, the philosophy of our culture."

But Manuel was also restless, competitive, and ambitious. There was little opportunity in Puerto Sábalo for a young man consumed by a desire to get ahead. At the age of seventeen, he left the vereda to seek work along the banks of the Caquetá.

"Where I come from, the only jobs going are illegal ones," he says. "If you have to transport drugs, collect coca leaves, or mine for gold, that's what you have to do."

He took the toughest, most dangerous job going.

The mining barges that ply their trade on Colombia's Amazon tributaries are rickety contraptions. The smaller ones consist of a pair of lanchas lashed together with planks, a tarp thrown over a log frame for shade against the sun and rain. The larger ones look like two-story houseboats, made with the same wood-panel walls and zinc roofs as the houses on stilts lining the river. In these craft, the top deck is given over to cabins and kitchens, and the crew might work on the river for weeks at a time.

The machinery is on the bottom floor. A large pump acts to suck sediment from the riverbed through a wide hose and into the body of the barge. There it passes through a grinder and then a sluice box, breaking down the material and separating out the finest grains. To these grains, mercury is applied to form an amalgam with the contained gold, and the resulting mixture is squeezed between a cloth and blasted with a blowtorch. If in luck, a miner is then left with a few small nuggets of molten gold.

Before any of this, however, the nozzle of the suction hose must be poked into the silt of the riverbed, ten meters or more below the surface. This is the diver's job. Manuel remembers the day when, still a teenager, he donned the rudimentary diving suit for the first time, only half-understanding the instructions given to him in Portuguese by a burly Brazilian.

A weight belt was strapped around his waist, and a long hose that terminated in an oxygen compressor was inserted into his mouth. He held the wider sediment hose with its metal-grill aperture, and jumped in.

Through his mask, visibility was never more than a few feet. He poked the nozzle of the hose into the silt, and waited to feel a tug on his oxygen hose. On deck, the Brazilian pulled on the hose to direct him where to go next, "like a donkey." Suspended in the water, tied by string to his mask, was a sock containing a hefty quantity of mashed garlic and ambil. It was meant to ward off large fish and boa constrictors.

Manuel worked for four years as a diver. A standard riverbed shift lasted two hours, but sometimes, if there were no other divers available, he would work a full seven hours. Over the years, dozens of young Indigenous divers had died due to faulty equipment, had been sucked away by strong currents, or had been trapped under overhanging rock formations. But it paid well, and Manuel excelled in the role. In recognition of his ability, the army once called upon him to search for the body of a drowned soldier.

Later, he worked a string of odd jobs along the Caquetá: sometimes as a logger; others, he preferred not to talk about. In 2016, he was arrested and bundled into a Black Hawk helicopter on one of the military's periodic raids of the illegal mining industry. It was a case of mistaken identity, he insists, as he'd been out of the mining game by then.

That year, Colombian authorities identified sixty-five illegal mining barges on the Caquetá River alone. Media reports claimed that armed guerrilla groups were sourcing more of their income from gold than from cocaine, and environmental agencies announced that Colombia's rivers had become some of the most mercury-polluted in the world. Manuel could sense the writing was on the wall for the gold business. His instincts were sound: the following year, the Colombian military launched a major operation against the industry, blowing up dozens of dredges and making mass arrests.

By 2017, he was already planning to return to Puerto Sábalo, he says; but, before that, he agreed to one more job on a Brazilian barge. It was a favor for an old friend who needed experienced hands on deck. In the long afternoons, when the heat of the day receded and the machinery fell silent, he found himself chatting happily with the girl who served him bowls of fish, plantains, and rice.

He told Magdalena Mucutuy of the life he wanted to build in Puerto Sábalo, and offered her the chance to be part of it.

"I told her that I was willing to help her out as much as I could, that I was going back to my hometown," says Manuel. "I didn't have a wife, and she was still young. We got together."

Fatima had wasted no time finding a job for her daughter following her thirteen years in La Chorrera. In Araracuara the bars were full and there were new motorbikes lined up outside. Anyone could see that the gold industry was on the up. Fatima had heard grumblings that one of the Uitoto girls on a Brazilian barge couldn't cook anything that the whites could stomach. She pulled some strings, and Magdalena took the job.

"She worked well on the barge," says Fatima. "With the money they paid her, she was able to buy new clothes, and she put on weight, she got her body back."

It was three months later that the first words of complaint

found their way back to Fatima. Magdalena was spending her afternoons on the barge sitting and joking with one of the workers, the one they called Carramán. The manager couldn't ignore it any longer.

"Magdalena was always cheerful, and she had this big, cackling laugh," says Fatima. "My friend called me up and said, 'She doesn't want to work anymore.'"

Given her objections to her daughter's previous living conditions in La Chorrera, it seems that Fatima hoped Magdalena would find a wealthier partner in the mining industry, but she insists that she tried to warn her off Manuel from the start. His fondness for alcohol and cannabis were common knowledge, she says.

"I told her, 'Magdalena, Manuel will only bring you problems. He's a stoner, and your two daughters are delicate. Magdalena, you have to think with that head of yours!' But she didn't listen to me, she didn't obey me anymore."

Once again, Magdalena defied her mother. Manuel was physically strong, and commanded the respect, and sometimes the fear, of his peers. In a violent and uncertain world, he seemed to offer a promise of security. But he was also articulate, persuasive, and funny. He was confident, as assured singing in his native language in the maloca as he was speaking into the microphones in Spanish later, when press interest in the search for the children was at its height.

Above all, however, Manuel was ambitious. In a community where the lack of opportunity caused many to lose hope, he gave the impression of someone who would never quit until he made it. Magdalena, a twenty-seven-year-old single mother with two children in tow, allowed these traits to drown out her mother's warnings. In March 2019, she gave birth to Tien, her son by

Manuel, and they moved to Puerto Sábalo.

Four years later, when he called her from Bogotá and laid out the logistics for her, she was willing to follow him once again.

After their meeting at the shop, when Magdalena had deposited a bag and received the letter from Manuel, Martha didn't see Magdalena for a week. It was Lesly who came to the counter each day, shy and well-mannered, to buy the food the family needed for cooking. On one occasion, she brought Tien with her, and they ate ice cream on the porch among the gaggle of soldiers scrolling on their phones, rifles slung over their shoulders.

Magdalena's first attempt to board the cargo flight had been thwarted by money. Superintendent Jeison Castro had accompanied her in the shade of the Antanov's wing as men loaded white sacks full of giant catfish into the belly of the plane. He remembers the pilot telling Magdalena that he could not accept passengers who did not pay the full fare.

"I told him, 'Come on, man, let us have a couple of seats from the goodness of your heart, it's a humanitarian thing.' But he wouldn't budge," recalls Castro.

But Magdalena had money, according to Manuel. He claims he left her 15 million pesos before he left Puerto Sábalo. It appears that, having failed to acquire the free humanitarian flight her boyfriend had told her she was entitled to, she was reluctant to admit she had the funds. The figure that Manuel cites, equivalent to almost US$4,000, might be inflated, but it's clear that when the cargo plane returned seven days later, on April 25, Magdalena offered cash to pay for her family's transit.

"No, she's not going," Superintendent Castro recalls the pilot saying. "The order is that she cannot leave."

In different circumstances, in an environment less complex than the one she lived in, Magdalena would still be alive. She and her family would have landed in San José del Guaviare on April 25 on board a cargo flight. The reasons for denying them boarding were initially mysterious. Superintendent Castro, never one to underestimate the extent of the guerrillas' influence in the town, assumed that they had put pressure on the airline. He had taken down Manuel's testimony two weeks earlier, and believed that the family were targets, too.

Manuel, on the other hand, blames Fatima.

"Her mother called [the airline], telling them not to allow my girl and the children onto the plane," he says. "Fatima was always opposed to her daughter going out with me. She cursed her own daughter."

On April 30, Martha saw Magdalena for the last time. She was wearing a white T-shirt with a red rucksack, and she was in a hopeful mood. A chartered Cessna 206 was due to land at 2.00pm and to depart shortly after for San José del Guaviare. Magdalena was confident that this was her ride out of town. It was time to say goodbye, but before she left, Martha opened the camera app on her phone. At the first attempt, Magdalena covered her face with her hand, but Martha was insistent. The second photo showed Magdalena smiling, looking down at Cristin as she crawled on the countertop. It was the last photo taken of Magdalena Mucutuy alive.

That afternoon, the family waited in the shade in front of the army base. Superintendent Castro handed Lesly his cell phone, which was playing the Super Mario Brothers movie. The three children, gathered in close, seemed captivated by the tiny screen.

Shortly after 5.00pm, three hours behind schedule, the tiny Cessna 206 touched down, its landing gear kicking up clouds of dust. It taxied back along the runway and parked on the small patio of concrete in front of the military base. The pilot opened his door and kicked down a small ladder. His feet were barely on the concrete when Superintendent Castro approached him and began to explain the situation. But the pilot shook his head and pointed to the sky. The sun was low, veiled by the steam haze of the jungle canopy. It was too late to fly.

As she watched the policeman and the pilot opining about the weather, Magdalena stood with her back to the passengers as they disembarked from the plane. She didn't see the queasy, haunted expressions on their faces. She didn't see them shake their heads as they collected their bags from the Cessna's undercarriage and tried to wipe away the traces of oil.

A little over an hour later, Martha heard a knock on the door. Outside was someone she hadn't seen for a decade. Captain Hernando Murcia's hair was thinner, his cheeks a little more jowly, and he seemed to have lost the jovial expression she remembered. He asked her if she could put him up for the night, and Martha showed him through to a room at the back of the shop, where he dropped off his pilot's bag. Then he sought out a bar of soap, and promptly began to wash his damp and wrinkled pilot's shirt— white, with black-and-gold epaulettes—in the outside sink.

Those who knew Hernando Murcia say that he was proud of his position. He had always enjoyed the prestige and trappings of being a pilot. But that pride glowed even stronger now, at the age of fifty-five, given that a few years previously he had feared his career was over.

In 2019, Murcia had found himself driving a taxi and selling *empanadas*, the local fried pastries, outside the airport in Villavicencio. For much of the twentieth century, the city of Villavicencio had been the last stop on the Andean road down from Bogotá. To the east lay expanses of plains stretching 650 kilometers to the border with Venezuela. To the south lay the vast Amazon jungle. The city's tiny airport was the only link to the settlements in these distant regions, and their populations were dependent on a small cadre of rough-and-ready bush pilots to deliver food and goods to them, and to ferry the sick to safety.

Murcia viewed himself in this tradition. Over the course of a thirty-year career, he'd racked up over 10,000 flight hours, mainly at the controls of the Douglas DC-3, the Second World War–era propeller plane that had found a second life as the cargo vehicle of choice in Colombia's cash-strapped aviation sector. It was a dangerous job. In the park outside the airport, close to Murcia's empanada stand, a large gray cement plinth, adorned with golden wing insignia, lists the names of 230 fallen and disappeared airmen. They were the unsung heroes of Colombia's development.

In the 2010s, the DC-3 was largely phased out, and Murcia's job went with it. His income from selling fried foods and driving was barely enough to support his wife and two daughters. But in November 2019, he'd had a lucky break. An old colleague put in a good word for him with a new company flying a couple of old Cessnas to remote regions of the Amazon.

The company was called Avianline Charters, and its owner, Fredy Ladino, was proud of its achievements. Since its foundation in November 2018, he says, the company had flown over 20,000 people, many of them medical emergencies.

"[We've picked up] people missing a hand, with their hand in a plastic bag … women giving birth in our planes because the Indigenous don't have any other way of getting out. We're the only ones who go there."

Ladino is in his early forties, barrel-chested, with a short
military haircut and bright white teeth. When I meet him in his
office, in a hangar at the end of Villavicencio airport, he recounts
the day when Murcia, asking for work, sat in the seat I am now
occupying.

"He looked like a homeless," says Ladino, "But I knew he
was a very, very good pilot. These days, there are only seven pilots
in Colombia who can land on the toughest landing strips, and
Murcia was one of them."

Murcia took to the skies again. Over the course of the next
four years, he ran some of the most difficult routes, battling regular
storms, improvising landings on short, bumpy airstrips. Even by
his own standards, however, April 30 had been a harrowing day.

With his shirt drying on the line, Murcia wandered into the
kitchen and took a seat at the table. He asked for fish—the same
fish, if possible, that he had eaten on his last overnight stay, a
decade before. He was crestfallen to discover that fish had been a
rarity on Araracuara's menus for several years. Martha slid a bowl
of meat with plantains in front of him.

"Then he began to talk and talk," she says.

Murcia had left his home in Villavicencio at dawn that
morning. He'd flown five passengers to San José del Guaviare, the
last commercial airport en route to the jungle, before making a
450-kilometer round trip to Cararú, in the eastern Amazon. On
his return, he'd topped up with thirty-seven gallons of fuel, and at
1.00pm he'd set off for La Chorrera. So far, so good.

But on the two-hour flight south, thick black clouds had
loomed towards the windshield—a terrible hurricane, he said, with
thunder and lightning, which seemed to come out of nowhere.
He'd chosen to arc around the storm, adding thirty minutes to his
journey and using up valuable fuel. When he'd finally landed at La

Chorrera, a further dilemma had lain in store. Under the palm-roofed structures that flanked the runway, his three passengers were waiting, but the fuel he was expecting was not. The locals told him that the man responsible for supplying the fuel was still recovering from the previous night's heavy drinking.

Murcia had two more trips to make that day: first to Araracuara, where he would pick up a team of consultants working on forestry projects, and then back to San José del Guaviare. He made his calculations, and judged he had enough fuel to complete the first. He made some calls. A pilot friend agreed to let him use the fuel he had stashed with Martha for emergencies. He made the decision, and ordered the passengers aboard.

The flight to Araracuara had been hair-raising. Afterwards, passengers said that the Cessna had been making strange noises and felt underpowered. They arrived, safe but shaken, far too late to attempt the onward trip to San José de Guaviare. Even Murcia seemed rattled, Martha thought, as he slowly picked at his plate.

She listened to Murcia's story the same way a barman might listen to a late-night drinker's tales of woe. When he was done recounting the day's tribulations, he slipped into marital problems. His wife, he told her, resented having forgone her own professional career to raise their daughters. When he flew the DC-3, money hadn't been a problem; they had even had enough to hire a maid. Flying the chartered Cessnas meant an irregular salary, and Murcia wanted to ensure a good education for his daughters. It had been necessary to tighten their belts.

Finally, he perked up. He began to regale Martha with tales of his beloved DC-3, its beautiful elliptical wings, the heavy rumble of its dual engines.

"He loved those planes, and he missed them," says Martha. "He said that flying those small little planes just wasn't the same."

When he was done eating, Murcia stepped into the back patio and looked up at the sky. A canopy of bright stars stared back at him. It was a clear night.

"Thank the Lord," he said to Martha. "Tomorrow is going to be a good day."

The bedroom she had prepared for him was small. At the foot of the bed, a child's pink bike rested against stacks of cardboard boxes. Overhead, a tiny picture of Jesus in a small oval frame was the only thing adorning the wood-paneled wall. He undressed and lay in the bed. It was then he realized that he'd broken a strict habit: he hadn't called his daughters to wish them goodnight. His phone was dead, and he couldn't find his charger. He turned off the light, and resolved to call them in the morning.

CHAPTER FIVE

Mayday

On the morning of May 1, Martha Muñoz woke at 4.30am and went to the kitchen to prepare scrambled eggs and coffee. Captain Hernando Murcia joined her shortly after. He was in a good mood, she noted, well turned out in his white shirt, and he wished her a happy Workers' Day. His phone had died overnight, and Martha lent him a charger so that he could power up his phone while he ate breakfast. His thoughts were with his daughters, Martha remembers. He told her that he always called home before takeoff.

Around 5.30am, Nestor Andoke, a local hunter, was crossing the runway as dawn broke. A few puffy clouds glowed orange in the morning light. On the square of concrete outside the military base, he saw Captain Murcia making his 360-degree check of the aircraft. Murcia kicked the tires, pulled on the propeller, and unsheathed the long metal dipstick to check the oil level. He pushed the wing flaps up and down, and then the rudder from side to side. At his feet stood three 12-gallon bottles of fuel. Nestor watched as Murcia climbed a stepladder and poured the contents into the tank on the top of the Cessna's right wing.

Around this time, Santiago Buraglia woke in his hammock, which had been strung up in the kitchen of a small house next to the runway. As he rubbed his eyes, he saw Magdalena Mucutuy lead her children through the kitchen to the back of the house. There was the sound of a tap being turned on and of water gushing into a bucket. Then he heard Magdalena and Lesly giving instructions to the younger children as they took their morning bath.

Buraglia hadn't expected to stay the night. He was tall and angular, with long hair and a goatee beard, and he worked as a consultant for Yauto, the carbon-bond company. The previous day, he had waited at the airstrip for the chartered Cessna that was supposed to ferry his research team out of the jungle. The plane had arrived late, however, and then a gray-haired policeman had approached him, explaining the situation. There was a woman and four children who needed to fly out. It was a humanitarian mission, he said. There would only be space for one of the four Yauto employees on the original manifest, and Buraglia had taken it.

He slipped out of his hammock and stood up groggily. The previous night, he'd spent four hours drinking beers and chatting about politics with Herman Mendoza on the porch of the house. Herman was a renowned Indigenous-rights activist, a thickset fifty-seven-year-old Uitoto with neatly combed-back hair and a disarming grin. He had been traveling on the Caquetá River to advise the local communities about how to negotiate the best deal with the carbon-trading schemes. But now he was in a rush to get back to Bogotá, where he had a meeting the following day. Sinking the dregs of his last can, Buraglia had agreed to let Herman to take his place.

When Magdalena and the children finished bathing, they returned to the kitchen, where the house's owner, Doña Irís, cooked them breakfast. They barely spoke, and, as he watched them eat, Buraglia thought they looked worried. He shared Martha's concern about what would become of them in the capital.

"I thought to myself, *These poor kids have to leave their territory, leave everything behind, to live in a rough neighborhood in Bogotá,*" he remembers. "You could see from their faces that they didn't know what the future held."

After breakfast, Magdalena shyly accepted his help with the luggage. He shouldered the red rucksack and walked with the family towards the army base. There, he hugged Herman goodbye and sat down on a rock to wait for the plane to take off.

He watched as Magdalena stood under the wing of the Cessna and spelled out the names of her children while Murcia wrote on his clipboard. One by one, the passengers picked up their luggage and stepped onto the electronic scales. The three adults and four children weighed less than 300 kilograms altogether. There was an additional 50 kilograms of luggage. A Cessna 206 is designed to carry loads of up to 500 kilograms, so weight was not a problem.

Nor was fuel. There were fifty gallons in the tank—more than enough to reach San José del Guaviare.

As he completed his tasks, Murcia glanced anxiously at his phone. He was beginning to run late. Buraglia recalls that he started to hurry the passengers aboard. Herman slid through the pilot's door into the copilot position. The family entered through the door at the tail of the Cessna. Magdalena and Lesly took the middle row, directly behind the pilot. Tien and Soleiny were at the rear.

"The pilot told them to get in quickly, and he closed the door," recalls Buraglia. "But then they waited ten minutes without taking off. I thought that was strange. Then I saw the pilot get out, rub a cloth on the windshield, and start looking at the engine."

As he watched Murcia fiddle around the front of the plane, he couldn't help noticing his expression. He seemed angry, or frustrated. Eventually, Buraglia gave up waiting for the flight to depart, and returned to the house where Doña Irís was preparing another batch of coffee.

"That pilot looked really grouchy today," he remembers telling her.

Murcia returned to the cockpit and started the ignition. The plane started to inch forward from the patio, but it advanced only a few meters before juddering to a halt.

Superintendent Jeison Castro heard Murcia call for help.

"The plane was stuck," he says. "There was a little hole in the concrete that the guy hadn't seen. These planes have small wheels, and he couldn't get it out."

Together with a couple of colleagues, Castro pushed at the wing struts until the Cessna pulled clear of the pothole. The whole thing took less than five minutes, and when he was done, he returned to his post behind the sandbag walls.

The Cessna taxied east down the runway, towards where the old US army base had been. Murcia made a neat 180-degree turn in the gravel. He revved the engine and pushed the throttle. The engine growled, and the plane accelerated.

It had not traveled forty meters when the left wheel fell into a deep groove in the gravel surface, causing the plane to veer sharply to the left and come to a sudden stop at the edge of the runway. An army corporal came running down the track towards them.

"When I arrived, the right wing of the plane was pointing down the runway. It had made a full ninety-degree turn, and it was jammed in a big hole," he remembers. "It didn't have enough power to get out of it. The right wheel looked wonky."

The corporal asked Murcia if it wouldn't be better to fly the next day. He replied that it would be fine, that he just needed a few men to help him right the plane. The passengers disembarked as half-a-dozen soldiers jogged over to lend a hand. It needed all their muscle and grunt to push the plane out of its rut.

As he caught his breath on the runway, the corporal turned to Magdalena.

"If something like that happened to my plane, there's no way I would get back on," he said.

But Magdalena dismissed his concerns. The problem was the terrible runway, she said—the plane would be fine.

Just after 7.00am, at the second attempt, HK-2803 took off from Araracuara airport. The corporal watched it go with concern.

"He ate up practically the whole runway," he remembers. "Normally, with a plane of that size, they get airborne before they are even halfway along."

At the end of the strip, close to the gorge with its population of macaws, a local woman was washing clothes. She ducked instinctively as the plane flew overhead. It was flying too low, and made a *ra-ta-ta* sound as it passed. She turned to her husband and said, "That plane is going to fall."

The inside of a 1982 Cessna 206 has the feel of a family hatchback car. The six leather seats are crammed together, the transponder looks like a dashboard radio, and a black gyroscopic compass hangs where the rear-view mirror should be.

The controls are startlingly analogue. Three twisting knobs— black, blue, and red—control the power, the revolutions per minute, and the fuel flow to the engine. A gray switch adjusts the angle of the wing flaps. There are more electronics in a calculator. The relationship between a Cessna pilot and his plane is closer to that of a cowboy and his horse than it is to a commercial pilot and a Boeing 767.

"Murcia flew with his ass," says Fredy Ladino, the owner of Avianline. In pilot-speak, this is the highest compliment.

With no warning systems, the pilot is forced to rely on his feel for the plane. He has to use all his senses: as well as keeping his eyes on the gauges, he must listen to the sound of the engine and keep his nostrils open for the smell of oil or burning. He has to feel the vibration of the engine, transmitted through the seat beneath him to his backside.

Over the course of his long career, Murcia had developed a toolbox of bush-pilot skills relevant to the region. He had learned to read the weather—in particular, the clouds. Contrary to popular opinion, it was not the dark ones you had to fear, but the tall white ones. When he reached his destination, he might fly over the runway, tilting the aircraft to catch the reflected sun on any puddles lying in wait, or observing the formation of cattle at nearby ranches to account for crosswinds. Cows always face away from strong winds.

He also kept a mental log of conditions at each landing strip in the Amazon. All of them have a reputation. Some were simple grass clearings, where the foliage could slow takeoff speed. Some were dirt strips that became greasy in the rain and caused landing equipment to hydroplane. Others had seen their lengths drastically curtailed by giant potholes caused by previous heavy landings. But even experienced pilots balked at making the trip to Tomachipán, where the half-constructed airstrip was a hazardous mixture of concrete slabs and grass. Murcia was one of the very few who flew the route.

There were some things beyond a pilot's control, however. On the dashboard of the Cessna 206 there are almost a dozen gauges, but two of them are the most important. When the temperature of the engine rises and the oil pressure falls, it means an engine failure is imminent. Ten minutes after takeoff, at an altitude of 8,500 feet, Captain Hernando Murcia saw the pointers of each gauge resting in the red zone. He picked up the radio handset.

At the control tower in Villavicencio airport, there was the buzz of static and a voice that tried its best to hide any trace of panic.

"Mayday, Mayday, Mayday, 2803, Mayday, Mayday, Mayday. The engine is idling, I am going to look for a field."

The air traffic controllers located HK-2803 on the radar, and less than a minute later they informed Murcia that there were two airstrips close by where he could make an emergency landing. There was no response. The Cessna was flying over a notorious communications black spot, and had fallen out of radio contact. The controllers contacted another light aircraft flying in the area, and requested it act as a radio bridge between the control tower and HK-2803. Still there was no response.

Fifteen minutes later, Murcia's voice returned to the radio.

"2803, the engine has powered up again. I am 120 nautical miles from San José, rising to 8,500 feet ... 2803, six people on board and autonomous for three hours."

The air traffic controllers allowed themselves a sigh of relief. A few minutes later, when Murcia radioed in again, they were assured that disaster had been averted.

"At the moment, I'm 109 nautical miles from San José with good visual conditions. Request to maintain 5,500 feet." The Cessna had lost 3,000 feet in altitude, but the problem with the engine seemed to have been resolved.

But only moments later, Captain Murcia once again saw the needles of the temperature and oil gauges flick suddenly into the red. He realized that there was only one option left to him.

In the jungle, there are two places to perform an emergency landing: in a river or on the treetops. Crashing in the river risks flipping the plane and drowning your passengers, but it is the much-preferred option. Landing in the forest canopy is the stuff of dark aviator jokes.

Harry Castañeda, another Avianline pilot, no longer finds those jokes funny. Less than two years earlier, in July 2021, he had flown HK-2803, the very same plane, on a medical mission to the eastern Amazon. Not long after taking off, with a doctor and passenger on board, he smelt burning. He banked the plane and headed for the nearest runway, a distant strip of brown dirt visible beyond the trees.

"It's a terrifying situation," he recalls. "I was flying, brushing against the canopy of the forest, and there was a small hill between me and the landing strip, and I knew we weren't going to make it because the plane was losing power."

As the plane lost altitude, he tried to restart the engine, and then—exercising impressive foresight under pressure—he took a photo of the temperature and pressure dials, using his phone's camera. Then he headed for a point where the treetops seemed thick and level. He dropped his speed and pulled the nose up, almost stalling the plane over his chosen spot. At the last moment, he pushed his seat back, put his legs in the space between himself and the copilot's seat, and braced for impact.

Castañeda and his passengers walked away from the crash. He had performed a near-perfect treetop emergency landing. The plane had glided along the treetops for fifty meters before coming to a complete stop. Only then had it pitched forward and down towards the earth, the impact of the thick branches of the trees against the wings acting to slow its descent before it crashed, nose-first, into the forest floor, forty meters below.

The impact with the dashboard opened up a wide cut on the left side of Castañeda's forehead, but his decision to swivel his legs into the center of the plane had prevented them from becoming trapped in the wreckage. His passengers were unharmed, and, with the GPS system he kept on board, Castañeda was able to guide them through the jungle to the nearest Indigenous settlement, five kilometers away.

The subsequent investigation ruled mechanical failure as the cause of the crash. The photo of the dashboard's gauges helped Castañeda avoid blame and potential hefty legal fees. There was significant damage both to the plane's engine and fuselage, but it was too valuable to leave it to rot in the jungle. Over the next week, a team of men made its way to the crash site, disassembled the Cessna, and carried its component parts to the riverside. Bit by bit, HK-2803 made its way back to Fredy Ladino's hangar in Villavicencio airport. It passed an inspection by the aviation authorities, and returned to operations with Avianline in March 2023, just two months before Magdalena and her family set foot aboard.

In July 2023, Manuel Ranoque sued Avianline Charters for damages, claiming that HK-2803 had not been fit to fly. Ladino argues that the plane was in good condition, pointing to its successful inspection by the Colombian Civil Aviation Authority (Aerocivil). It's common, he says, for planes to be repaired and returned to service after an accident. Besides, he'd had little other option.

Ladino says that he had wanted to expand Avianline's fleet, but had been met with an insurmountable problem. In Colombia, the Cessna had become an endangered species. Straightforward to fly, hard to detect on radar, and with the ability to land on airstrips the length of soccer pitches, the Cessna had long been the drug traffickers' aircraft of choice. Pilots were offered a year's salary to deliver a single cargo of cocaine to ports in Venezuela or Suriname, where the planes were often abandoned. Legitimate operators couldn't compete with the dealers for the scarce second-hand Cessnas on the local market.

Ladino maintains that his mechanics did an excellent job in patching up HK-2803. He argues that the crucial damage to the aircraft happened on the runway at Araracuara.

There's something else that a bush pilot needs to have, aside from the ability to fly by his ass. In the industry, they call it criteria.

The life of a Cessna pilot in the Colombian Amazon is full of endless small decisions, many of which he must make alone. When he wakes, he has to look at the sky, compare it to the frequently unreliable weather forecasts, and decide whether it's safe to fly. On his morning inspection, he must decide which imperfections on his aged vehicle—wonky tires, missing rivets, damaged flaps—must be dealt with immediately, and which can wait until he gets back to the hangar. In the cockpit, he needs to judge whether a shower can be flown through or would be best skirted around. He must choose which spots on landing strips are less terrible to put down on than others.

But bush pilots also need soft skills and emotional intelligence. Above all, they must be capable of saying no to other people. To bosses whose livelihoods—but not lives—depend on getting people and products from one place to another at the agreed time. To passengers who simply *must* reach their destination. To cargo dispatchers who weigh their packages with less-than-reliable scales. A pilot must be able to put his foot down when the circumstances don't meet his criteria. A pilot in good standing knows he can do so without risk to his job.

But Hernando Murcia was not in good standing.

His peers say that Murcia was at the bottom of the list of Avianline pilots, the one who flew the least. In the cliquish world of bush pilots, he was something of an outcast. His awkward behavior and attempts at humor earned him the nickname "*Chiste malo.*" ("Bad joke.") People who did take the time to talk to him soon found themselves listening to long monologues about extraterrestrials or Adolf Hitler. None of this helped him rise up the ranks.

At home, money was tight. He had a wife and two children to care for and he couldn't afford to turn down a gig when it presented itself. During the Covid-19 pandemic, when other pilots refused to pick up sick patients without proper safety gear, Murcia went willingly, wearing only a facemask.

"He was the backup for all the pilots, the Plan B," said José Miguel Calderón, who had flown Piper Senecas with Murcia. "If a pilot couldn't fly because the plane was bad or the weather was bad, or if he didn't feel safe, or if he was tired, the company called [Murcia], and he said yes to everything. His criteria were very low."

A pilot's day is full of tiny decisions, but they are rarely fatal. Every so often, however, they can compound and spiral. Captain Murcia had been a pilot for thirty years, but on May 1, 2023, his lack of criteria caught up with him.

One year after the event, Aerocivil's investigators had still not determined the reasons why HK-2803 went down. Having heard the story of the missing fuel supplies in La Chorrera from passengers on the harrowing flight the previous day, many paisanos in Aracurara believed the Cessna had simply run out of gas. Nestor Andoke, however, had seen Murcia refill on the runway and a pilot subsequently confirmed to me that he had agreed to let Murcia use the emergency fuel he had left in Araracuara. Some locals said it was the fault of the rundown airstrip; others blamed the plane itself. Fredy Ladino, the boss of Avianline, puts it down to human error.

On his laptop, he shows me photos of the propeller, taken from the wreckage of HK-2803 in May 2023. There are white scratch marks on the tips of each blade. He maintains that these were not caused by contact with the treetops, which he said would have bent the tips back, but had been sustained earlier that day. He believes that the propeller made contact with the ground when the Cessna swerved off the runway at the first attempt at takeoff. That impact reverberated along the shaft, damaging the engine.

"The factory says that if the propeller touches anything, even a sheet of paper, you have to take out the motor and check it, because it's so delicate," he says. The correct course of action would have been to send the engine back to the manufacturer for a detailed analysis. He says that his pilot's decision to break from protocol was born of empathy. Murcia was a Colombian bush pilot who took his duty to the community seriously. He believed that the lives of Magdalena and her family were at risk in Araracuara, and made their transit his priority.

"The poor guy thought, *I need to do something*, and it was his urge to help that brought on the error, that caused the accident," says Ladino.

The corporal's testimony from the runway also suggests that Magdalena was unfazed by the failed takeoff; perhaps Murcia understood this as a determination to leave the jungle.

But Magdalena was not a frequent flier. Given the constant grumblings in town about the state of the runway, it seems likely she assumed that such accidents were a routine occurrence, leading her to underestimate the severity of the incident.

Ladino's theory doesn't explain earlier events, however. Passengers on the previous day's La Chorrera–Araracuara leg had said the plane felt underpowered. Several witnesses also saw a concerned Murcia fiddling with the Cessna's engine well before he taxied onto the runway. The plane had lacked the power to extract itself from the small pothole in the concrete outside the army base.

Murcia may have been concerned for the safety of the family on board, but it's also possible that he was worried about his job. That morning, he had received WhatsApp messages from management demanding to know the reasons for his delay in taking off. No pilot wants to earn a reputation for tardiness. Perhaps it was professional pressure that led him to underestimate the severity of the problem he had identified in the engine and to neglect his criteria.

A final, perhaps most probable, cause for the crash was suggested to me by a Cessna pilot. In high Amazonian temperatures, the oil in the Cessna's engine expands and excess oil is ejected from the engine via a drainage system. Frequently, a small amount of ejected oil finds its way into the storage unit under the belly of the aircraft. But passengers from the previous day's flight to Cararú reported that when they recovered their luggage, the bottom of the unit was thick with the stuff. The engine could have been suffering from an oil leak.

The fact that Murcia's engine restarted after a stiff drop in altitude supports this theory. At high altitudes, where the temperature is cooler, oil contracts. The engine is starved of oil, causing a motor failure. As Murcia's plane rapidly lost altitude, falling from 8,500 feet to under 2,000 feet, the engine would have heated up rapidly, causing the oil inside to expand and fill the engine once again, giving the impression that the problem had been resolved.

That day, with the power returning, Murcia flew past Cachiporro, a tough airstrip in the middle of nowhere, aiming for the second back-up option—a better runway in the bigger town of Miraflores. It was a fatal misjudgment.

At 7.43am, the pilot's voice was heard once again at the control tower in Villavicencio.

"Mayday, Mayday, Mayday, 2803, 2803, the engine has failed again … I'm going to look for a river … I have a river here to the right." A minute later: "103 miles outside of San José, I am going to land …"

In the cabin, Captain Murcia shouted out orders to his passengers. He instructed Magdalena to open the rear right-hand-side door, next to where Soleiny was sitting. They were going to land in the river. They had to get ready to abandon the aircraft as soon as they touched down on the water—there would be a window of only a few seconds before the water entered the cabin and dragged the aircraft into the depths. The rear door would be their escape route, but Soleiny and Tien didn't know how to swim.

It is Ladino's contention that this represented a final error on Murcia's part. Even now, after the constellation of misjudgments that had led to this desperate moment, there was still a chance for him to save himself and his passengers. If Murcia had dropped his speed and attempted a treetop landing, the adults on board could have survived, Ladino says, but Murcia was determined to make it to the river. The opening of the rear door and the fact that he didn't turn his legs into the middle of the aircraft, as Castañeda had done two years earlier, suggest it was never his intention to flop the belly of the Cessna into the canopy. He went in too fast, and the impact of the nose hitting the branches was so great that it knocked the engine clear of the Cessna—something that would not have happened at a lower speed, according to Ladino.

Magdalena returned to her seat. In front of her, Murcia was gunning the engine and fighting with the controls, but up ahead the brown curls of the river were sinking from view behind the tree line. Through the window, she watched the canopy rise up to meet them, until, from the carpet of green, individual trees and then branches became distinguishable. There was the rapid-fire sound of foliage thwacking against the wings, and a loud thud. The noise of the engine disappeared completely. The Cessna tipped forward violently and plunged nose-first towards the forest floor.

PART II

FORTY DAYS

CHAPTER SIX

An Upside-down World

When Lesly Jacobombaire Mucutuy came to, she felt the weight of her body hanging forward and the pinch of the seatbelt around her waist. She heard the sound of dripping. She opened her eyes.

Below her, the back of the black leather seat was slick with blood. Above, just a few inches from her face, were the mud and leaves of the forest floor. She reached her right hand to her forehead and felt the contours of a long, open gash that stretched along her hairline.

She struggled to make sense of her upside-down world. To her right, a triangle of white metal jutted towards her through the smashed window. It was the trailing edge of the plane's wing. A few shards of glass protruded from the window frame; beyond them there was only green. If she craned her neck, she could see the roof, caved in like a crushed soda can.

And when she turned to the left, she could see her mother, slumped forward in her seat, one arm dangling towards the ground, her long hair draped over her face. Terrifyingly still.

The dreadful memories began to arrive. Her mother reaching across to tighten her seatbelt. The pilot fighting the controls, yelling panicked orders to the passengers. The hands of the heavy-set man in front of her desperately searching—on the dashboard, on the door frame—for something to brace against. Then the deafening thud and the stomach-churning sudden descent.

"Mama?" she whispered. Then, louder, fear cracking her voice: "Mama?"

But she already knew.

Something in Magdalena's posture, the terrible inertness of her arm, the way her chin jutted towards the ground, told Lesly that her mother was dead.

Lesly hung there, upside down, staring at her mother. She felt her chest tighten and, above that, her stomach clenched. The first waves of panic and nausea began to course through her body.

Then she heard the muffled, desperate cry of a baby.

From the folds of Magdalena's body, still cradled by a rigid arm, Cristin's plump leg emerged.

Lesly struggled with the unfamiliar buckle around her waist. When it surrendered its grip and she fell forwards onto the ground, her left leg remained trailing behind her, and she let out a yelp of agony. Her seat had come off its rail, and her calf was pinned between the metal frame and the floor. She pulled and twisted until her heel eased its way out of the collar of her sneaker and her foot was released. A searing pain spread through her leg.

She crawled towards her mother. Beneath her, next to where she placed her hands, the pilot's white shirt seemed to glow in the dim light. The back of his head protruded from the mud.

On her knees, Lesly reached out a hand and pulled at Cristin's ankle. Her eleven-month-old sister slid from her mother's clutch, gasping and crying. Lesly hugged her tightly to her chest. She looked up. From the back seats of the plane, two small faces looked back, silently.

Lesly got to her feet in the narrow aisle, brushing up against her mother's body as she did so. Her left leg buckled beneath her, and she grasped the seat for support. Keeping hold of Cristin with one hand, she pulled herself up to sit on the back of the seat she had been traveling in. As she worked to release Soleiny and Tien from their seatbelts, they began to cry. She looked at each child. Soleiny was bruised on her head and her chest, but Tien was unscathed.

Next to Soleiny's seat, the rear door of the Cessna hung open, swinging gently on its rear hinge. Lesly went first, lowering herself by her arms as far as she could, then letting go before landing painfully on the forest floor. She got to her feet and supported her weight against the plane's wing, reaching up to receive Cristin as Soleiny passed her down.

Once Soleiny and Tien had clambered out of the plane, they retreated a few meters into the forest, in the shadow of the aircraft's bright blue belly. It was only then that Lesly could fully make sense of what had happened.

The Cessna's fuselage rose up vertically, as straight as the forest trees, its blue-tipped tail sticking out like a flag on a mast. The cockpit was entirely buried, and the crumpled wings were bent backwards, flush with the forest floor. Ten meters away, a hunk of metal the size of a refrigerator spat and hissed in the damp foliage. It was the Cessna's engine, knocked free by its collision with the treetops, the anatomy of its pistons and wiring now exposed.

Behind the plane was a thick-trunked palm. Lesly sat with her siblings at the base of the tree. Tien asked her why their mother wouldn't wake up but Lesly didn't know what to say. Soleiny stared at the side of Lesly's face, where the blood ran thickly from the wound in her forehead. Lesly knew from her mother that open wounds, in the heat and humidity of the jungle, needed to be treated quickly. But that would require a return to the plane.

She propped open the swinging rear door of the plane with

a branch, and hoisted herself up. She remembered that the passengers' luggage had been stored in the space at the back of the plane. On the side of Tien's seat, she found a small lever that popped the seat forward. She pulled out the bags and dropped them through the plane door. Behind them, attached to the fuselage, was a small yellow box with a flashing light. Next to it was a black square zippered bag with a red cross that Lesly instantly recognized. She grabbed it.

As she was about to leave, she noticed, on the lowest reaches of the cabin, two plastic bottles of water. She lowered herself to where her mother's body rested, and retrieved them. She tried to pull her shoe free from under the seat, but it was stuck fast.

By the time she returned to her siblings, Lesly was already formulating a plan.

First, she needed to stem the bleeding. She removed one of the diapers from Cristin's bag and pressed the absorbent material to her forehead. She held it in place using gauze from the plane's first-aid kit. Next, she draped a towel over the lower branches of a nearby tree to create shade, and hung up the mosquito net she had found in the luggage. The children crawled inside. Lesly knew that someone would come looking for them. How long that might take, though, was a different matter.

They waited.

The heat rose. From her position, Lesly could see that a swarm of flies had converged around the plane. She understood what it meant, and when Tien became restless and wanted to return to the plane to check on their mother, Lesly held his wrist fast. From the diaper bag, she removed Cristin's bottle and one of the sachets of Klim powered milk that lay alongside it. She emptied half the sachet into the bottle and poured in some water. Cristin grasped the bottle with both hands and began to suck greedily.

Then Lesly retrieved the pair of *copuazú* fruits that her mother had packed the night before. They were brown and hairy, each the size of a papaya, but once she removed the outer skin, the flesh below was white and succulent. There were dozens of large seeds inside, each encased in a film of flesh. She gave a seed each to Soleiny and Tien and then took one herself. It tasted like chocolate.

For two days and two nights, the children remained in the shelter. The rain fell in sheets. At night, when the temperature dropped and their damp clothes pressed against their skins, the children huddled together for warmth. Lesly lay on her back ,with Cristin on her chest to keep her out of contact with the cold forest floor. They ate the second copuazú, and finished the last of the water.

On the third day, Lesly awoke to the sound of rustling coming from the plane. Without waking her siblings, she slipped out from under the mosquito net and limped in a wide arc around to the left-hand side of the plane.

A vulture, with jet-black wings and a head of grey, wrinkled skin, was poking its way around the base of the plane. Lesly hated vultures. The swarm of flies had grown, and she smelled the sour odor of decay for the first time. Soon, she knew, the jaguars would come.

As she returned to the shelter, she understood she had a decision to make. They had waited two full days, but no help had arrived. She couldn't be sure that the planes she had heard were looking for them, or whether anyone was coming for them at all. They couldn't stay next to the Cessna, with the smell of the dead growing stronger.

Lesly resolved that they had to try to find a village. La Chorrera, Araracuara, and the other riverside settlements she knew were always next to water. She remembered the pilot's panicked words into the radio handset. *I'm going to find a river.* She had seen, over the shoulder of the man in the cockpit, the brown coils of a river through the windshield.

Lesly looked at the position of the plane. Even nose-deep in the jungle, it was clear the direction it had been traveling in. She looked at the thick forest ahead of her, and felt the dim heat of the sun on her face. They would walk east.

CHAPTER SEVEN

Villavicencio

On the morning of May 1, Magdalena's estranged husband, Andrés Jacobombaire, was in a small park near his home in Suba, a working-class neighborhood on the north-western outskirts of Bogotá. He was performing the daily exercises prescribed by his physiotherapist. Holding the children's climbing frame for support, he stretched one leg slowly, painfully, in front of him and shifted his weight onto it.

Suba had once been home to the Muisca people, an Indigenous tribe that traded the maize and potatoes they grew in the rich soils of the highland savannah for emeralds and precious metals mined by neighboring peoples. The Muisca's reputation as accomplished goldsmiths attracted the attention of the Spanish conquistadors, and by 1538 they had been conquered, their survivors forced into a reserve. In the centuries that followed, Suba was swallowed up by Bogotá's expanding borders.

Today, it is a residential district, a grid of squat red-brick apartment blocks built to absorb waves of immigration from the countryside. In 1950, two-thirds of Colombians lived in rural areas. By 2020, three-quarters lived in cities. During this time, the internal conflict between the guerrillas, the army, and paramilitary forces forced many Indigenous to flee their ancestral lands.

Census data shows that between 1993 and 2018, the number of Indigenous people in Bogotá rose from 1,298 to 19,603. Many of them settled in Suba.

In the months after Magdalena's departure from La Chorrera in 2017, Andrés' health had deteriorated steadily. The town's only doctor, a recent graduate completing his mandatory year's service in the countryside, could offer him nothing but painkillers. By mid-2019, Andrés was bedridden, unable to move, and in December that year his sister, Rosamira, managed to raise the funds and fill in the paperwork required to move him to the capital for professional treatment.

When he had completed the exercises prescribed by his physiotherapist, he returned to the flat he shared with Rosamira. As he was making a sandwich, he checked his phone, and noticed he had a missed call from an unknown number. Then, as he settled down in front of the television to watch a movie, the phone rang again. This time, he picked up.

"Is this Andrés? Are you the father of Lesly and Soleiny Jacobombaire?"

The prim Bogotá accent and serious tone could only mean bad news. Andrés immediately began to shake. The man from the air force explained that his daughters, along with his wife, had been en route to San José del Guaviare when their flight had disappeared shortly after takeoff. It was too early to say what had happened, or if they were alive or dead, but a search-and-rescue operation had been established in Villavicencio. They would send transportation for him in the early hours of the morning.

Andrés hung up and changed the channel. On the news, a reporter was talking over a flight map showing the trajectory of the Cessna. The names of his wife and children appeared on the screen. He started to cry.

Andrés is forty-two years old, and at first glance appears fit and healthy. When we first meet, he is leaning against a brick wall dressed in sneakers, jeans, and a Led Zeppelin T-shirt. His dark hair is long and swept back on top, and closely trimmed around the sides. He looks like he could belong to a younger generation of paisanos, those who have grown up in the city and hang around the skate parks and rock bars.

That image cracks when he begins to walk. He is accompanied by his older brother, Jairo, who holds him firmly by the elbow and whispers encouragement in his ear. As he puts one foot slowly in front of the other, his face is tense with the effort. When we sit down to talk, Andrés' speech is slow and stuttering. At times, his eyes widen with frustration as the words fail on his tongue, and Jairo, protectively, steps in to answer questions on his behalf.

Andrés' memory is precise, however, and the emotions of the past are close to the surface. They often express themselves in his face before the words come out.

When the call came through, he hadn't seen Lesly and Soleiny for six years. With pleading eyes, he explains how he had tried to convince Magdalena to return them to him. He had offered to pay for their flights to La Chorrera and later Bogotá.

"I called her twenty, thirty times," he says. "In the end, I got tired of begging."

When Magdalena stopped returning his calls, he took solace in the fact that, once they reached the age of eighteen, the girls would be free to travel alone and visit him. On the night of May 1, as he waited at the entrance of his apartment block with Rosamira, he wondered if he would ever see them again.

At 3.00am, a black minivan pulled up outside. Rosamira helped her brother descend the stairs and enter through the sliding side door. In the back seat, Andrés felt a hot anger growing inside him. If Magdalena had heeded his calls, if the girls had been with him, he told himself, this would never have happened. But he was angry, too, at his own misfortune, at his physical condition that had prevented him from traveling to Araracuara to collect his daughters, that made it impossible for him to work and to provide a stable home for them in Bogotá, and that put him on the back foot in any confrontation.

Twenty minutes later, the door to the minivan slid open again. A man with dark skin and tightly curled hair stepped in, his woolen sweatshirt stretched over strong shoulders.

"*Buenos dias,*" he said, nodding towards Andrés and Rosamira. When they didn't respond, he took a seat a couple of rows in front of them. Andrés couldn't help himself.

"Are you Manuel Ranoque?" he said. He wanted to sound tough, but it came out in a stutter. The man turned and looked at him, first with confusion and then with slowly dawning recognition. He smiled and turned away again.

Rosamira squeezed her brother's hand. *Be calm,* she told him. Motionless on the outside, Andrés was burning with emotions. There was pain and anger and humiliation. But there was also fear. He, too, knew of Manuel's reputation. He wondered if he was carrying a knife. He regretted his outburst, and hoped, for the rest of the journey, that Manuel wouldn't say anything to him.

At Bogotá airport, Ismael and Diana Mendoza, the father and younger sister of Herman Mendoza, were waiting in the departure area. They boarded the air force plane in silence and arrived in Villavicencio shortly after daybreak. They were escorted to a hangar at the end of the runway, passed by a Cessna undergoing maintenance, and entered an office at the back, on the ground floor. The walls were adorned with framed photos of Fredy Ladino in aviator sunglasses, sporting a beaming smile and standing in front of an array of light aircraft.

The very man, but more tanned, approached them and shook them by the hand. He had cut short a holiday in Aruba to take command of the search mission. Fatima and Narciso Mucutuy, who had arrived from Chukiki, soon joined them in the office. Fredy invited them to sit in the plastic chairs. Andrés and Rosamira made sure they sat furthest away from Manuel.

Ladino stood before them and laid out the events of the previous twenty-four hours.

Radar data showed that the plane had veered north-east from its flight path at 7.44am. Flight analysts had extrapolated the direction of travel to identify a wedge-shaped initial search area stretching to the Apaporis River.

Within hours of the crash, Ladino explained, two Cessna pilots had made repeated flyovers of this area, but they had yielded no results. There was no sign of the plane, no glint of fuselage in the sun, no break in the tree canopy—just an endless carpet of green. A ground search was necessary, but there was a problem. The usual entities—the national search-and-rescue program, the Civil Guard, the Red Cross—were not yet ready to enter the area. It was too remote, and they couldn't guarantee their security, given suspected guerrilla activity in the region. Instead, Avianline would lead the search. Ladino had already sent men to the area, and the air force would be sending an AC 47 and a Huey helicopter later that day. The Avianline office would be the operation's base.

There are conflicting assessments of the first few days of the search for HK-2803. Andrés and Rosamira, who soon asked to receive their briefings in a separate room from Manuel, felt like they were in good hands. "Fredy was very attentive. He kept us updated, calling us every few hours, informing us of every detail," is how Rosamira remembers it. "I trusted him."

That view was not shared by the other relatives. Ladino's speech did not inspire confidence in Diana Mendoza, who had abandoned her nursing studies to attend the rescue operation. The relatives spent the night in a downtown hotel. The next day, Ladino told them he had lost contact with the search team. Diana had questions. What training did these rescuers have if they entered the jungle without suitable equipment? What use was sending more aircraft if the vegetation was too thick? Where were the professional organizations, whose entry Ladino insisted was imminent? But there was one question that gnawed at her. If a family of rich Bogotanos had disappeared in the Amazon, would the response have been so slow?

Manuel, in particular, was not a man accustomed to inaction. He demanded to be flown to the jungle to look for the plane himself.

"In Villavicencio, it was as if they wanted me to be sitting there, feet up, in the office or back in the hotel, eating a meal, out of the way," he remembers. "But for me, this was about my children—it made me uncomfortable."

That evening, Manuel and Diana Mendoza began to knock on the doors of people they knew in Villavicencio. They were human rights defenders, jungle experts, and members of the Civil Guard—anyone who might be able to join a search or help fund it. Next, Diana called her cousin Natalya in Araracuara to try to round up a team of hunters and trackers to enter the jungle. Finally, she called the OPIAC, the Indigenous rights organization where her brother worked, to ask for their advice. One name was at the top of their list.

Edwin Paky is a thirty-six-year-old agricultural engineer and cartographer with a straggly beard, thick-rimmed glasses, and a fondness for baseball caps. He is a Muinane, proud of his heritage, and, like his second cousin Herman Mendoza, a spirited activist for Indigenous rights. When I met him in Araracuara, he was dressed in gumboots and a khaki shirt with bulging chest pockets, having recently returned from an expedition gathering data for a forest carbon project.

On May 1, he had been in Plaza Bolívar, the epicenter of Colombian political life. Bogotá's central square is where Congress, the cathedral, and the courts face each other. That morning, he had stood with 600 members of the Indigenous Guard in protest at the Senate's blocking of a major reform package. The guard, a group of legally recognized security forces that operate in Indigenous communities, stood in rank and file, with their thick wooden canes, their *bastones de mando*, resting on their shoulders.

A year earlier, Gustavo Petro, a one-time member of a guerrilla group, had been elected president. He was the country's first left-wing head of state, and enjoyed the support of the vast majority of Colombia's Indigenous and Afro-Colombian populations. However, his party was a minority in the legislature, and his plans to overhaul the country's pensions, health, and labor laws in favor of the poor had ruptured his fragile coalition. The May Day march was intended to show popular support for his mandate. When it was over, the green and red flag of the Indigenous guard hung from the neck of Simón Bolívar, the national hero whose statue presides over the plaza.

Edwin Paky was member of a new generation of Indigenous Colombians who had studied at university, practiced a profession, and had the political nous to understand how the levers of power worked in the country. Two days after the protest, he was meeting with his activist companions when he received a phone call from the OPIAC.

"They wanted me to enter the jungle as an expert," he recalls. "I know the jungle, and I know how to handle certain navigation equipment, GPS, map analysis—that kind of thing."

Edwin had grown up in Araracuara, so he had a paisano's feel for the jungle, but he was also technology-savvy. In a previous role, he had led research teams to randomized GPS locations in the Chiribiquete National Park, just north of where the plane had disappeared. This combination of Indigenous know-how and technological expertise made him a natural choice to lead the search team Diana was hastily putting together. That evening, he had time to pack a small bag with a change of clothes, a mosquito net, and a razor before catching the afternoon flight to Villavicencio.

When he checked into the hotel where the relatives had been put up, he found Fatima and Narciso in a state of distress. "They were very worried because the search had given no results, and the whole process and the logistics situation were moving very slowly," he says. "We didn't have clear information about what was happening, and so the family were very flustered, they were desperate."

Delio Mendoza, Herman's younger brother, had also flown in from Leticia, the city on the border with Brazil. Together with Manuel, they agreed that they would join the search for their loved ones. On the runway at Villavicencio, a Cessna was being loaded up with supplies to send to the search teams. It wasn't much: some food, bottled water, and some machetes. Ladino, however, refused to let them step aboard.

"At the start, there were lots of obstacles," remembers Delio.

"They didn't want to let us enter the jungle, due to the dangers and other such excuses, that there were protocols to be followed. They kept telling us that the army, the firemen, the Civil Guard were making their best efforts, but were seeing no results. By May 4, we started to hear rumors that the search would be suspended. We felt that if we didn't go, they would have left my brother and the others lost in the jungle."

With the search for the plane into its fourth day, media interest was growing steadily. A small group of cameramen and journalists were camped outside the Avianline office, waiting for any update. Manuel was more than happy to share his thoughts. In the person of the desperate, determined father with the unfiltered speech, they found their main protagonist.

On 4 May, he told *Semana* magazine, "We don't want to sit here in Villavicencio anymore waiting for an answer. We want to be closer to our families, we want to them to give us this opportunity, and we demand that they include us in the search." He was ready to risk everything he had, he said, to hold his family in his arms again.

For now, however, Ladino remained unmoved. There was a simple reason why he could not allow civilians into the search area: the plane had crashed in the territory of the Estado Mayor Central, the most organized and violent guerrilla group in Colombia. To enter required tact and personal contacts. In this respect, he says, he held a vital advantage. Over the course of his career, he'd become friends with a handful of men who knew these corners of the jungle, had built relationships with the Indigenous populations, and knew how to handle the armed groups.

"The only people who could work in the zone were mine," he says emphatically when we meet in Villavicencio. "The army couldn't enter because they had detected guerrilla units on the radar."

Three months after the crash, and facing a fistful of potentially ruinous lawsuits, Ladino's bright smile and chummy demeanor remains undiminished. Having walked me through his own views on the reasons for the Cessna's crash, he is keen to go over the actions and efforts of the ground team he organized, to explain how close they came to success. Because, while he may be stuck behind a desk these days, Ladino likes to think he still has the instincts of a bush pilot. He knows how to get things done in the jungle, he says. He knows the right people to call.

He made contact with the guerrillas.

"They told me that we could enter to look for the [plane] without any problems. They authorized [my guys] to enter."

CHAPTER EIGHT

Casa Dumar

In the sea of green below, a single witness watched the final moments of HK-2803.

The river that Captain Murcia had desperately willed the Cessna towards, the river that had remained fatally beyond the reach of its wheezing engine, was the Apaporis. There are hundreds of major rivers in Colombia, but the Apaporis remains uniquely mysterious, with a sinister reputation all its own. Over the course of 1,000 kilometers, it thunders through canyons and gushes over huge waterfalls. There are points where it disappears completely, funneled through tunnels of stone.

Impossible to navigate by boat, the Apaporis remained beyond the reach of Spanish conquistadors and European explorers. When US biologist Richard Schultes ventured to the region in 1943 in search of natural rubber sources for the war effort, its basin was a blank space on the map. The People of the Centre believe that the Indigenous who inhabit this dark pocket of the Amazon are possessed of magical powers. The Apaporis was still slowly revealing its secrets well into the twenty-first century. When a team of scientists ventured to the region in 2019, they found thirty-six new species. "It's pristine jungle, the most remote and unexplored region of Colombia," says Nicolas Castaño, a member of that expedition.

Yet on the banks of this remote stretch of river there was a single small house. It had wooden walls, four rooms, and a zinc roof. A tiny solar panel stood on a pole in the garden. The house's owner lived there with his family and a couple of laborers in almost complete isolation, a seven-hour boat ride upstream from the nearest Indigenous settlement. He was known as Dumar, and no one who received his hospitality in the coming weeks ever remembered hearing his first name. Discretion and a certain level of anonymity was important in his line of work.

Behind the house, an expanse of forest had been cut back. On one small section, Dumar's wife grew manioc, plantain, and fruits. The larger part of the land was given over to the cultivation of the only economically viable crop in the jungle: coca leaf.

Across the Colombian Amazon, there are hundreds of tiny, secluded operations like Dumar's. The leaf is harvested, bagged up, and sold to men on lanchas who pay in cash and ask no questions.

It wasn't always this way. In the 1980s, Pablo Escobar's Medellín Cartel processed cocaine in secret Amazonian labs, but most of the coca was grown in the humid valleys of Peru and Bolivia, and flown in on light aircraft. The boom in Colombian jungle production was an unintended consequence of the US's "War on Drugs." In the 1990s, the Drug Enforcement Administration worked with South American air divisions to force down, or shoot down if necessary, suspected drug flights. The radar base at Araracuara and the fighter jet on the runway had been part of this program. In 2001, it ended in scandal when a Peruvian fighter shot down a civilian floatplane containing a family of US missionaries, but by then the geography of the drug trade had shifted.

Coca cultivation relocated to the Amazon, closer to the labs, and it had new bosses—the FARC. Taxing the trade boosted the guerrillas' finances and emboldened their operations. In 1996, FARC fighters captured the Las Delicias military base on the Caquetá River, 200 kilometers upriver of Araracuara. Within a week, the hundred-strong force of Americans abandoned the radar base, leaving most of their kit rotting in the sun.

A year later, Colombia overtook Peru and Bolivia to become the world's top coca producer, and by 2022 it was estimated to control two-thirds of global production. International drug agencies estimate that over half of this production takes place in Indigenous territories.

On the morning of May 1, Dumar had been picking leaves on one of the higher points of his land when he heard a buzzing overhead. Looking up, he saw a small white and blue plane heading east a mere fifty meters above the forest canopy before he lost sight of it in the trees. He returned to his house, but decided against telling his wife what he had seen.

And when, two days later, a lancha docked at the small pier by his house, its occupants huddled under a tarp against the rain, Dumar offered greetings and hospitality. But he told them nothing about the plane.

The search for the wreckage of HK-2803 was undertaken, initially chaotically and with little coordination, by three disparate groups. Later, elite Colombian commandos would abseil from helicopters. Eventually, they would combine their efforts with dozens of Indigenous volunteers. In the first five days, however, the operation was coordinated by Fredy Ladino and performed by his friends.

The first group to arrive at Casa Dumar, as the riverside house became known, was led by Ferney Garzón. He was a trader who had built a business portaging construction materials past impassible rapids on the Apaporis. On the afternoon of May 1, he flew to the tiny Indigenous village of Cachiporro, the nearest settlement to the suspected crash site. He was known to the locals, who numbered fewer than forty in total and viewed him as a friend. He had no problem recruiting a team of six men to help the search, and the following morning they left on a lancha, headed upriver.

Garzón had answered Ladino's request for help, and had left his home in the eastern jungle in a hurry. He took no specialist communications equipment with him. As soon as his team left Cachiporro, they lost all contact with the Avianline operations center in Villavicencio. Fredy Ladino picked up his phone again.

In Mitú, a jungle town just forty kilometers from the border with Brazil, Andrés Londoño took the call. He was a tough, capable man, and he would play a vital role in the search for the missing Cessna. In September 2023, I met him in the café at Villavicencio airport as he was returning from a work trip. He was strongly built and dressed in a clean, white polo shirt, the most formal work attire that the jungle permits.

Today, his river transport company has a fleet of fourteen vessels, providing vital ferry services to the most remote Indigenous villages of the Colombian Amazon. But he started out seven years ago with a single lancha, taking tourists to the gigantic falls of Jirijirimo on the Apaporis. It was during this time that he started up a professional relationship with Fredy Ladino.

"Andrés, you've got to help us out," he remembers Ladino saying over the phone in May 2023. "You know the territory, you know the people, and you know how to handle the delicate security situation."

Londoño took the news in his stride. He knew that the odds

of finding any survivors were slim, but he was used to being called upon for grisly tasks. When someone drowned in the river or was attacked by an alligator, the local authorities often tasked him to find and recover the corpse. During the pandemic, he'd zipped up the body bags of countless Covid-19 victims. In his years navigating the distant tributaries of southern Colombia, he'd seen enough death to instill in him a respect for the jungle and an admiration for the people who lived within it.

Londoño isn't Indigenous—his parents moved to the Amazon from the rolling hills of Colombian coffee country in the early 1980s—but he's married to a Uitoto woman, and he has had close contact with the tribes and clans of the forest. Their culture has rubbed off on him. He views the jungle with a paisano's eyes, and when he got the call to help with the search, he knew to take precautions. He told Ladino that he would need two seats on the Cessna to Cachiporro.

"The jungle has many mysteries," he says in his matter-of-fact way. "I went with a shaman—someone who could help me navigate, someone who could provide their cultural protection."

The shaman was called Hector. Londoño had first met him in his tour-leading days, and had been impressed as much by his spiritual connection to the jungle as by his ability to navigate and find food and water. By the early afternoon of May 3, the two men sat side by side in the Cessna, surrounded by food parcels, bottles of gasoline, and an outboard motor. They took notes on the terrain and the shape of the Apaporis as the aircraft circled over the search area.

When they landed at Cachiporro, they found only women, children and the elderly. The young men had departed with Garzón's group. Londoño attached the outboard motor they had brought with them to the last serviceable lancha, and set off for the seven-hour journey upriver. They arrived at Casa Dumar just after 1.30am on May 4, where they found Garzón's crew.

At dawn the next day, the men convened in the largest room of the house. Dumar's wife served them casabe and coffee. There were half-a-dozen Indigenous from Cachiporro, including a former guerrilla who had demobilized in 2016. Then there were Garzón and Londoño, a trader and a lancha operator respectively, and Hector, the shaman from a distant tribe. Dumar's son and two of his laborers, who worked the coca fields, were added to the group. This ragtag search team was the first to enter the jungle in search of HK-2803.

Londoño laid out the maps he had brought with him on the dusty floorboards. Looking over his shoulder, Dumar helped orientate him. He aligned the maps with the rivers and the hills he knew so well. Then he calmly listed the potential predators they might meet: jaguars, anacondas, wild boar, hornets. Then there were the mosquitoes and flies, which carried malaria, yellow fever, and leishmaniasis, a skin-eating disease. The search team listened in silence. "There may also be landmines," chimed in the ex-guerrilla from Cachiporro, who had a sense of where the FARC had deployed their munitions.

Equipped with this sobering knowledge, the men packed their bags. It wasn't much: some plantains and *fariña*, a granola-like grain made of manioc, supplied by Dumar's wife, some smoked fish, and half-a-dozen old machetes they had found in Cachiporro. This time, however, they had a communications system. Londoño had a Garmin GPS, which not only pinpointed his position but allowed him to send and receive messages to and from the Avianline base in Villavicencio. They also had a target. Fredy Ladino sent through some coordinates that lay a half-day's trek south from Casa Dumar. They were the best hope of finding the plane.

The yellow box that Lesly had seen behind the rear seats of the Cessna was an Emergency Locator Transmitter (ELT). Activated under sudden impact, such as a crash, the ELT sends out a 406 MHz radio signal every twelve hours with the aircraft's registration information and its approximate location. Modern ELTs incorporate GPS data, and are accurate to around 120 meters. But the one onboard HK-2803 was an older model. It sent out three signals in the first thirty-six hours, and each was several kilometers away from the others.

At 7.00am, the men rode the lancha south and disembarked on the west bank of the river. They waited on the shore while Hector walked over to the trees, bowed his head, and performed a quiet ritual. The People of the Center reserve the deepest reverence and respect for the jungle. Before any expedition into the monte, permission must be granted from the spirits that reside there. For the Indigenous hunter, entering the jungle to obtain food is not a right; it is a diplomatic process, requiring negotiation. As such, it is best approached with tact and humility. A successful hunting trip speaks more about the generosity of the spirits than the skill of the hunter.

Hector asked the spirits of the jungle to permit them entry and to dispel dangerous predators from their path. When he returned to the group, the men from Cachiporro unsheathed their machetes. Between the trees, there was a tangle of thick vegetation: shrubs, ferns and hanging vines. Hacking a path with diagonal swipes, the men entered the jungle.

Within minutes, their shirts were soaked through with sweat and clinging to their bodies. Many of the trees were over fifty meters tall, and their crowns were so dense that they shut out the sky. At ground level, the foliage was unrelenting. In the half-light, the men made slow progress. Each slash of the machete, each step

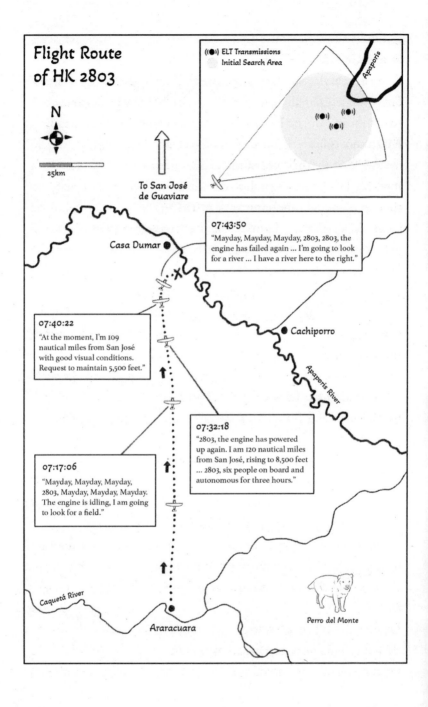

Flight Route of HK 2803

N

25km

To San José de Guaviare

ELT Transmissions
Initial Search Area

Apaporis

Casa Dumar ●

07:43:50
"Mayday, Mayday, Mayday, 2803, 2803, the engine has failed again ... I'm going to look for a river ... I have a river here to the right."

Cachiporro ●

Apaporis River

07:40:22
"At the moment, I'm 109 nautical miles from San José with good visual conditions. Request to maintain 5,500 feet."

07:32:18
"2803, the engine has powered up again. I am 120 nautical miles from San José, rising to 8,500 feet ... 2803, six people on board and autonomous for three hours."

07:17:06
"Mayday, Mayday, Mayday, 2803, Mayday, Mayday, Mayday. The engine is idling, I am going to look for a field."

Caquetá River

Araracuara

Perro del Monte

forward, was earned in sweat, and soon swarms of wasps arrived, attracted to the smell.

"The jungle there, it just eats you up, it turns you yellow," Londoño says of that first day. "It was dark, we were exhausted, but the mind won over the body. We knew that with each passing hour there was less chance of finding them alive."

At 2.00pm, they heard the drone of an aircraft. Garzón got it in his head that they should start a fire to alert the plane to their presence. Some members of the group protested, but he went ahead anyway, lighting smaller twigs and then throwing damp branches into the flames. A plume of dank smoke filtered up through the canopy.

They pressed on, and by late afternoon they were approaching the coordinates. Florencio Tamborrero, one of the men from Cachiporro, smelled it first—above the fetid musk of the forest, the sour odor of decomposing flesh. It was mixed with another smell: fuel.

Londoño fished his lighter from his pocket and struck the flint. The flame leant slightly to the south, bent by a barely perceptible breeze. They set off to the north, and picked up the pace. Fifty meters on, he struck the flint again. This time, the flame flickered in all directions.

"We didn't know where to go," recalls Tamborrero. "The wind kept changing directions, running around like a dog."

As the men looked about desperately for signs of the plane or for a break in the canopy it may have opened up, they heard the first rumble of thunder. The rain drummed lightly on the leaves, then it fell in droves. The smell was extinguished entirely. Londoño checked his watch. It was almost 5.00pm. In the forest, darkness falls suddenly, so with it the risk of losing his own team members increased dramatically. He set a bearing for Casa

Dumar, and the team pulled in close, in touching distance of the man in front, as they grimaced and turned their heads away from the stinging sheets of rain.

That night, as the rain drummed steadily on the zinc roof and the men made their beds on the floor of Casa Dumar, Londoño checked the data on his Garmin. They had covered fifteen kilometers, but his body felt like it had walked three times as far. On one of the maps, he noted the area where the smell had been strongest. They could cut down their walking time if they took the boat a little further downriver, he decided.

The next day, they boarded the lancha. Above them, the sky was a murky gray, with thick clouds backlit by the pale morning sun, but from their position in the middle of the Apaporis, they had a view over the treetops. And several kilometers away, to the south, they saw black shapes hovering above the canopy. They dove out of sight and rose up again—vultures.

The lancha pulled over on the opposite bank. One of the men from Cachiporro tried to climb a tree in the hope of getting a better view of the area over which the scavengers were circling, but the rain was already coming down. They had no ropes, and the bark of the tree was slippery in his grip. Meanwhile, Fredy Ladino was sending through new coordinates for his team to search. Londoño felt divided about the new order. His hunch was that the vultures were hovering close to the point where he had smelled the decomposition the previous day. That didn't necessarily mean the plane was nearby—it could have been the carcass of a tapir or a jaguar—but he was sure he'd smelled fuel.

He stuck to his orders. The team once again returned to Casa Dumar, battling against a downpour. Londoño noted that many of the men were coughing, and some were complaining of intense headaches. He was concerned it might be dengue. If the conditions improved, Londoño told himself, he could lead a team back to the target area the following day.

But on Saturday May 6, the Avianline search team was disbanded. Fredy Ladino sent through news that Colombian Special Forces troops were preparing to enter the jungle. They would be on a combat footing, expecting contact with the guerrillas, and any case of mistaken identity could be fatal. The team's responsibility now was to help clear a section of the jungle to create a makeshift heliport for incoming choppers.

Ladino knew, however, that the men from Cachiporro, not least the former guerrillas, would not stick around once the soldiers arrived. Seven years of "peace" had done little to warm their views on the military.

"These were tense days in which my people had to escape, run to a lancha, and disappear," remembers Ladino. "The Special Forces were entering—they had come to clear the area."

Londoño rode with the team in the lancha back to Cachiporro. As he watched the waters rush by, he could tell that his companions' hopes of finding the plane had been exhausted. Each passing day lessened the chance of finding survivors. As they passed the search area, he looked to the sky. There were no vultures. He wondered if he'd been mistaken.

The next day, Londoño flew home to Mitú, but he would return a few days later to help construct the heliport. A week later, when the Cessna was found and he checked its coordinates against his own GPS records, he felt his heart sink. On his first day in the jungle, when he had struck his lighter to detect the source of the smell, he had been less than 300 meters from the battered chassis of Cessna HK-2803.

CHAPTER NINE

Apaporis

In the afternoon, as the children rested against a tree, Lesly rolled up the muddy cuff of her jeans to expose her left shin. Her ankle was badly swollen, and purple bruises had spread up along her calf. That morning, she had discarded her one remaining shoe at the crash site, and now walked on in her socks. She carried Cristin in her right arm. In her backpack were the key items she deemed vital for the journey to the river.

Inside were the baby's bottle with its powdered milk, Cristin's diapers, a battery-powered flashlight, and a pair of scissors. There were also plastic water bottles, two cell phones, some rolls of gauze from the medical kit, and an envelope containing the children's civil registry documents. In the days before their departure, her mother had made a great fuss about the envelope, so she assumed it was important and kept it with her. It was light, after all. It was the weight of the towel and the mosquito net, both damp from the rains, that caused the thin, cheap straps to cut into her shoulders.

Over the course of that morning, the pain in her left leg grew worse with every step. As she led Soleiny and Tien eastwards through the jungle, she became ever more dependent on the trees to support her weight. She steadied herself by pressing her hands against their trunks, pulled herself up by low-hanging branches, and leaned her hip into high buttress roots. Where there was nothing to support her, she handed Cristin to Soleiny, and crawled on her hands and knees.

As she inspected the bruises on her leg, she felt her sister's eyes on her. Soleiny's expression, usually so cheery and animated, was one of fear and concern. Lesly beckoned her over to sit between her legs. She tugged at Soleiny's blue hairbands and ran her fingers through her hair, doing her best to remove the mud. As she pulled the pigtails back into place and tightened them, she told her sister not to worry. The river was close.

An hour later, Lesly heard the sound of flowing water, and soon she caught a first sight of the brown waters of the Apaporis through gaps in the trees. She quickened her pace, forgetting the pain. It was a little over three kilometers from the wreckage to the river, but it had taken them most of the day. Now the sun was low in the sky.

On the riverbank, Lesly looked upstream and downstream. On either shore, as far as the eye could see, there was nothing but jungle. There was no cutaway in the tree line that might signify the entrance to a village, no footpaths rising from the river to the crest of the shore, no wooden posts that a lancha could be tied to. Above her, the sky was thick with clouds that were growing darker in the fading light. There was no sign, and no sound, of human life.

She hobbled over to the water and sat on a rock that was half-submerged in the shallows. She removed the plastic bottles from her backpack and filled them where the water ran clearest. As the bubbles rose from the neck of the bottle, a shimmer of silver movement caught her eye. Holding still, she studied the water. A *sabaleta* fish, five inches long, flickered through the water below her.

Higher up on the riverbank, Tien and Soleiny watched their

older sister staring, motionless, at the water. Lesly knew several ways to catch a fish. In Puerto Sábalo, she had spent many a lazy afternoon in the hull of a tiny dugout canoe with her friends. With a simple rod and line, a lead sinker, and a hook baited with bits of chicken skin, she had caught plenty of sabaleta. But there was no hook in her backpack, and nothing that could be used for bait.

She recalled that, when she was five or six, she had gone to the long lagoons behind the family chagra in La Chorrera with her grandfather and her sister Angie. Her grandfather had carried a bucket of barbasco, the root of a native plant that had been beaten with a stick into a fibrous pulp. When he waded into the lagoon and sloshed the barbasco in the water, it created a great milky cloud. It stunned the fish, which came flopping to the surface and could then be picked up by his granddaughters' nimble fingers. Lesly remembered that the barbasco was a thick shrub with long oval leaves and yellow berries. She tried to remember if she had seen one that day. She hadn't.

Then she thought of the men who hunted for catfish in the waters below the rapids at Araracuara. They would walk along long bamboo platforms that jutted out from the boulders on the riverbank, wait patiently for a catfish to pass underneath them, and would then hurl their harpoons into the water.

Lesly searched the shores for a broken branch that was long and thin enough for her task. When she found it, she pulled away strips of bark at one end until the tip resembled a shard—not perfectly pointed like an arrow, but sharp enough to do the job. Sitting on rocks, higher up, Soleiny fed Cristin from her bottle. Tien watched his sister stand motionless in the shallow water, with all her weight on one leg, like a crane.

Lesly stabbed at the water several times, without luck. But she was patient, and she soon learned to adjust her aim to take into account the refraction of the water. After half an hour, Soleiny and Tien saw her raise the stick out of the water, to reveal on its tip a silver fish flapping in the dying light.

When she had three small fish, the children sat together on the rocks. Lesly wished they could build a fire and grill them on sticks, but in her search of the plane she had found no matches and no lighter. Instead, they dug their fingers into the fish and pulled out thin chunks of cold flesh. Lesly took a bite. It was slimy and sour, and it made her stomach turn. She watched Tien grimace and spit as he swallowed the meat. Soleiny shook her head. But Lesly insisted that both of them eat until the bones had been picked clean.

That evening, as she lay under the mosquito net, with Cristin on her chest and Soleiny and Tien curled up next to her for warmth, Lesly heard grunting. She recognized the sound: a tapir had come to the river to drink.

As the other children slept, Lesly thought of Puerto Sábalo. She thought of the small school on the hill with its two rooms, a handful of textbooks, and an anatomical skeleton in the corner. On Friday afternoons, she would finish her work as quickly as possible and pester her teacher to let the class leave early.

Behind the school was the open monte. Half an hour along a jungle path was a small freshwater canyon where they would cool off in the heat of the day. Lesly would impress her friends by swimming against the current. On one occasion, the children were surprised by the arrival of a drove of wild forest pigs. They hid in the water, among the floating logs, until the sniffing and snorting beasts went on their way.

She loved the canyon and the afternoons she spent there with her friends. It was the place they went to when they wanted to get away from their parents. And it was surrounded by fruit trees. There was the juan soco, the camu camu, the acai berries. The children would forage on the leafy floor to find the fruits. Sometimes the boys would climb the trees to knock them free from the branches.

Her plan to find help on the river hadn't worked. Now Lesly knew she would have to find food in order to keep her family alive. But in this new, strange jungle, she had found none of the plants she knew from her childhood. Eventually, she fell asleep to the sound of the Apaporis.

The next morning, Lesly fed Cristin with the last of the Klim. She wrapped the gauze from the first-aid kit around her head to create a bandage. Using a branch as a staff, she walked the banks until she rounded a bend of the Apaporis. Once again, looking upriver, she could see no signs of habitation, nothing that made her believe she would find any kind of rescue on its wild banks.

She remembered something she had heard from her grandfather, or maybe it was her teacher: the paisanos of the Apaporis were different from the People of the Center. They worshiped different gods and lived in the middle of the monte, in the dense forest.

It seemed like her only hope. She gathered her belongings, and led her siblings back into the jungle.

If the children had waited a little longer on the banks of the Apaporis, they would have seen the lancha.

CHAPTER TEN

The General

At 11.00am on May 6, two Black Hawk helicopters took off from the air force base at San José del Guaviare. In the back of the first one, members of the Dragon 4 commando team inspected their M-16 automatic rifles, tugging on the magazines and peering through the sights. Then they took their Italian pistols from their holsters and pulled back the top slides to load a round into the chambers. At the far end of the helicopter's belly, a bald and broad-chested sergeant fastened a grenade launcher to the barrel of his heavy machine gun. When they were done, seven faces, pinched between Kevlar helmets and thick chinstraps, turned to their captain.

Those faces could have belonged to taxi-drivers, barbers, or construction workers. They were the sort that wouldn't warrant a second glance if they passed you in the street. In contrast to the muscle-bound and tattooed images of US Special Forces troops, the men of the Joint Special Operations Command (CCOES in its Colombian initialization) are almost universally inconspicuous. But they are the most elite troops in Latin America, with unparalleled combat experience in some of the world's most hostile climates.

"The Special Forces are the guys with the capacity to go deeper and further in a high-threat environment," says General Pedro Sánchez. "Not only can they combat threats, but they can guarantee their upkeep, their communications, and their logistics." When I first meet him in September 2023, he has been commander of the CCOES for just under a year. He is fifty-one years old, with a youthful, handsome face and a physique honed by regular 5.00am CrossFit sessions. He is the first air force general to lead Colombia's elite combined Special Forces unit, and proud of the fact; in his Bogotá office, he wears the brown bomber jacket of his former unit. But there is also something self-effacing, almost bashful, about his demeanor. He pauses to consider my questions, and speaks with a soft, slow voice.

In the three days since the Cessna had disappeared, the military had been on standby. A costly deployment could be avoided if the air reconnaissance could find evidence of the crash site, or if the Avianline ground team could locate the wreckage in the jungle. Shortly before midnight on May 4, however, General Sánchez was woken by his phone.

"Prepare some units," General Elder Giraldo Bonillo, the head of the Colombian armed forces, told him. "You're joining the search for the light aircraft."

Since the day the Cessna disappeared, Sánchez had suspected that his troops would be called into action. The remoteness of the crash site and its history of guerrilla activity meant it was too dangerous for regular soldiers, never mind civilian rescue teams. That left the CCOES, and he was confident that his men were up to the task. It would be a straightforward operation—in and out. A welcome change of pace to the usual missions, the "catch-or-kills."

The CCOES's office in Bogotá has the feel of the corporate

headquarters of an unglamorous company. White drywall intersects with faux-wood flooring and glass doors. Behind them, vacant office chairs face huge whiteboards scrubbed meticulously clean. The only thing breaking the atmosphere of corporate sterility is a glass cabinet stretching along the side of one corridor.

Its walls are crammed with framed photos of muddy-uniformed men, standing and kneeling with arms around each other like pub soccer teams. The base of the cabinet is stacked with souvenirs and loot: old ammunition boxes, epaulettes bearing FARC insignia, a beret with a Che Guevara pin, and what appears to be a brown felt voodoo doll. In the final section of the cabinet, the most recent photo is of a thickset bald man in profile, one side of his face pressed into the mud and leaves of the forest floor. This is the CCOES's trophy cabinet.

For decades, the Colombian special forces were best known for busting armed groups and rescuing hostages.

"The CCOES was created to go after strategic objectives, the heads of the FARC and other armed groups," says Sánchez. "We neutralized the main leaders and forced the FARC into peace negotiations."

In the 2000s, when the FARC threat was at its highest, the Colombian armed forces held the respect and admiration of a large portion of the population. A 2011 Gallup poll found that 85 per cent of Colombians had a favorable image of the armed forces, making it the most trusted public institution in Colombian life. Backed with US finance and newly acquired Black Hawk helicopters, the CCOES eliminated top guerrilla commanders in daring parachute raids in the most remote corners of the country.

A popular soap opera called *Hombres de Honor* (*Men of Honor*) portrayed fictional troops battling against guerrillas and narcos, liberating grateful villagers from tyranny, and rescuing beautiful female journalists from captivity. Many of the men enrolled in the CCOES admit that the show inspired them to sign up.

However, by 2023, the army's reputation had hit rock bottom. In the wake of the 2016 peace deal, the Special Jurisdiction for Peace (JEP), the body established to investigate crimes during the Colombian internal conflict, laid bare the atrocities that the army had committed.

They included the gang rape of a thirteen-year-old Indigenous girl, the sale of weapons to criminal gangs, and the indiscriminate bombing of dissident positions that left scores of children dead. Most damaging were details of the *falsos positivos* scandal. In February 2021, the JEP revealed that the army had killed at least 6,402 civilians and arranged the corpses to make them look like enemy combatants, in order to receive cash bonuses. In May 2023, as the commandos were preparing to enter the jungle, Salvatore Mancuso, the leader of a paramilitary death squad who was now in a US prison cell, was preparing to give testimony about the extent of the military's collusion in his group's massacres of innocents in the 1990s.

Following his election in June 2022, Gustavo Petro moved swiftly against the military. He appointed a human rights lawyer as his minister for defense, and sacked forty generals linked to the *falsos positivos* scandal and other corrupt practices. General Sánchez was one of the new faces brought into replace them.

"The concept of human security means that success lies not in the number of dead, but in substantially reducing deaths and massacres, and increasing substantially people's liberties and rights," the president said. What to do with an army that had grown bloated and privileged under his predecessors? For Petro, the answer was clear. They had to be deployed in humanitarian missions.

But when Sánchez awoke on May 5, there was little indication that the search for HK-2803 and its passengers would soon become the largest and most high-profile civilian rescue mission in Colombian history. That day, he called a meeting. Air force representatives laid out the unsuccessful attempts to locate the plane with flyovers. Intelligence analysts updated him with the latest known movements of guerrilla groups in the search area. The meteorological team gave him the weather forecast: incessant downpours. Logistics experts proposed strategies to insert and supply a troop deployment. Then Sánchez packed his bags to fly to San José del Guaviare, where the command base for the military's search for HK-2803 was being set up.

"I told myself we'd find [the plane] quickly," he recalls thinking on the way to the airport. "We had the position from the Emergency Locator Transmitter, and we had plenty of advanced technology." He did not yet feel the pressure, the weight of that responsibility on his shoulders. He soon would.

San José del Guaviare lies 200 kilometers south of Villavicencio. It is the last sizeable city before the Amazon jungle begins. In September 2023, at the army base that sits alongside a wide sweep of the Guaviare River, I meet the first soldier to enter the jungle in search of the missing plane. Captain Edwin Montiel has a round, clean-shaven face and a medium build that seems to get lost in his gray camouflage fatigues. Now in his late thirties, he had entered the CCOES the hard way. Having failed to make the cut at officer school, he spent ten years as an infantryman in eastern Colombia, fighting guerrillas and armed drug groups in the plains and swamps, before he passed a punishing selection process in 2014 and entered the ranks of the CCOES. "I'd been frustrated before, but I'd chosen this life and, eventually, I got there," he says.

On May 4, Captain Montiel and his Dragon 4 squad had been soaring over the lush, green mountains south of Bogotá suspended from paragliders. Colombia's rugged topography means that commandos have to be ready to fight in a diverse range of extreme environments. They camp out in the fog and subzero temperatures of the Andes mountains, march across energy-sapping sand dunes in the dry heat of the northern deserts, and engage in the claustrophobic, close-quarter combat of urban warfare.

It's in the jungle that the Colombian commando earns his keep, however. The jungle has been the theater of the military's biggest victories and most bitter defeats. When Montiel returned to earth and sat down with his lunch in the mess hall at Tolemaida Air Base, he got a tap on his shoulder from a superior officer.

"They never tell you anything," he says, "They don't tell you where you're going, or which armed group you will be confronting. Operational security is tight." The only relevant question was to ask whether his team needed to pack for hot or cold weather. Hot weather, was the reply. A Hercules transport vehicle was already waiting on the tarmac.

The next day, when he and his team took their seats in the operations room at San José del Guaviare, Montiel felt his excitement building. In the Special Forces he had gained access to high-tech weaponry and had trained for high-altitude parachuting and frog-suited amphibious assaults. But this wasn't the main appeal of the CCOES.

"I'm fascinated by operation development, anything to do with planning," he says. "In the Special Forces, an officer stands out for his ability to plan and develop missions."

In the main operations room, men in uniform were plastering

the walls with maps, and wheeling in computers and monitors. In the side rooms, a wide array of technology was being prepared and linked up: GPS systems, satellite telephones, microwave radios, and motion- and heat-sensing technology. In the hangars by the airfield, maintenance teams were clambering over a pair of Black Hawk helicopters.

That afternoon, General Pedro Sánchez briefed the twenty-seven Special Forces soldiers and dozens of associated support staff. His voice was calm and precise as he pointed to locations on the map.

A Cessna 206 had disappeared 100 miles north of Araracuara, about halfway into its flight to San José del Guaviare. Three signals from the ELT placed the crash site in an area two to three kilometers west of a sharp bend in the Apaporis River. It was not known whether the people on board were alive, but air force reconnaissance flights had detected smoke from a point close to the riverbank.

The search area was a little over ten square kilometers, and it was divided into a grid. Two eight-man teams would be the first to deploy. Dragon 4, led by Captain Montiel, would be dropped several kilometers to the north of the ELT coordinates. Destroyer 1 would land to the east of the search area, close to the Apaporis, to investigate the source of the smoke. A third team would deploy later that day to the south. Ares 3 was a direct-action team made up of eleven men, several armed with heavy machine guns, and two Belgian shepherd sniffer dogs named Wilson and Ulises. Its task was to provide the main assault force should the first teams encounter the enemy.

Once on the ground, the teams would push towards the ELT coordinates in the center of the search area, searching each square of the grid en route. This strategy served two purposes: if any survivors from the crash had begun to walk away from the site, they would be easier to intercept; more importantly, by landing at separate points, it would prevent the force being surrounded by hostile actors in the region.

Sánchez shared the latest intelligence on guerrilla movements in the area, and outlined the rules of engagement. His men wanted to know if they were entering the jungle on a war footing or in a humanitarian capacity.

"I told them: both," recalls Sánchez. "I told them not to hesitate to fire back if they took contact or saw a threat, but also to exercise caution, because the lives of the passengers were of the utmost importance."

From the start, therefore, the details of the mission were foggy. The troops didn't know whether to expect combat or to find survivors. They didn't expect to be in the jungle for weeks. And they had little idea that the whole country would soon be scrutinizing their strategy and actions.

Half an hour after departing San José del Guaviare, the Black Hawk carrying Dragon 4 team touched down to refuel at the military base of Calamar, sixty kilometers to the south. The garrison had been designated as the intermediate operations base for the mission. Crates of supplies were being stacked, and soon a team of explosive experts would arrive, ready to deal with any minefields. If the commandos took contact from the enemy, it was to Calamar that they would be evacuated.

Its tanks full, the Black Hawk rose up once again and pitched its nose south. "From that point on, it was total jungle," says Montiel. "Total, thick jungle."

They flew under a clear, blue sky, but as they approached the insertion point, dark clouds loomed over their destination.

"It was strange," recalls Montiel. "The place we were headed was covered with dark clouds, heavy with rain. The sky all around was totally clear—it was just that one area where the clouds were thick."

It felt like an omen.

The Black Hawk hovered above the jungle, buffeted by the wind and the rain. The men of Dragon 4 threw their ropes from the bay doors and clipped in. The first moments of any jungle operation are crucial. Abseiling through the canopy is dangerous in itself: wet ropes can slip from one's grip; men and equipment can get tangled in the branches; but more importantly, a hovering helicopter betrays its location to any enemy in the region.

On this occasion, the eight men of Dragon 4 reached the forest floor without a hitch. Crouching, they watched and waited in silence in the rain, communicating only through hand signals. When they were convinced it was safe to do so, they moved in single file slowly to their first GPS location, keeping their weapons raised at the shoulder.

Even in these first minutes, it became clear that the terrain was exceptionally difficult. "It was a virgin jungle, an inhospitable jungle, a jungle that had never been trodden by a human being," recalls Montiel.

The vegetation at ground level was thick. The soldiers didn't carry machetes, as breaking a path would have made them easy to track by the guerrillas So they had to move carefully, deliberately, over the creepers and ferns, pushing slowly through the thickets of branches. Visibility rarely extended beyond ten meters, making it hard to see their companions in front and behind. Underfoot, there was a thick and consistent leaf cover, meaning footprints would be nearly impossible to find.

Montiel instructed the navigator to lead the team to the center of the first quadrant they had to clear. When they arrived, he remained in place with three men, in a sentry role. The other four men dropped their heavy equipment and started to patrol. They crept off on the diagonal, towards the corner of the grid. Then they patrolled the kilometer-long base of the quadrant and returned to the center. There they took over sentry roles, and Montiel and his companions completed the same pattern on the other side of the grid.

They repeated this process, creeping towards the center of the search area, until the light ran out. "From 5.00pm, it was practically dark because of the forest itself, which was so great, so thick, that no rays of light entered," says Montiel. He posted a sentry and made camp. Soldiers boiled water on small gas stoves, and poured it into sachets of dehydrated food.

Montiel radioed San José del Guaviare to report their movements and to receive their orders for the next day. Next, he heard the voice of Lieutenant Montoya, the leader of Destroyer 1 group. They had reached the location of the smoke, but had found no signs of the aircraft or survivors. Only later would they discover that the fire had been made by the Avianline search team.

The men from Dragon 4 strung their hammocks and nets, and took shelter from the rain and mosquitoes. They were disappointed, but not disheartened. It was only the first day. Tomorrow, surely, they would have better luck.

CHAPTER ELEVEN

The Girl in the Blue Dress

The Apaporis is a blackwater river. Fed by run-off from jungle soils, its waters are low in dissolved minerals and are acidic almost to the point of sterility. This makes the waters safe to drink, and several species of fish have adapted to inhabit the nutrient-poor environment. But the Indigenous know the blackwater rivers by another name. They call them Rivers of Hunger.

The acidic soils surrounding the Apaporis limit the types of tree that can grow there. Plant diversity is much lower than in the basins of whitewater rivers such as the Caquetá. Growing manioc requires far more nurture and care.

On May 8, as the soldiers from the Dragon 4 team crept silently through the undergrowth, an Indigenous search team led by Manuel Ranoque and Edwin Paky were hacking their way through the branches and vines several kilometers to the north of them. Manuel was disturbed by the new, more hostile jungle they were encountering.

"In the territory I come from, you find many types of wild fruit," he recalls. "But this monte was poor. We only saw a few seeds, many of them were poisonous—we couldn't find much to eat."

After several days of pressure, Fredy Ladino had relented

and agreed to fly the Indigenous family members to Cachiporro. Manuel Ranoque, Edwin Paky, and Delio Mendoza stepped onto the dirt airstrip on the morning of May 7. The Cessna they arrived in took off again almost immediately, and returned three hours later carrying five men from Araracuara who had answered Diana Mendoza's call for assistance.

This group was led by Henry Guerrero. Short and strong, with a thin moustache and a shock of black hair, he had a face that could turn from a serious frown to a broad smile in an instant. Among his team was Nestor Andoque, the man who had seen Captain Murcia filling up his aircraft on the morning of the crash.

Andrés Londoño was also in Cachiporro. Even though his own search team had been disbanded, he remained determined to find the plane. At the side of the dusty runway, he showed the new arrivals the areas he had searched, and put a cross over where his team had smelled the decomposition. As he prepared to board the Cessna, Manuel pulled him aside. He was convinced, he knew for a fact, he said, that his partner and children were still alive.

In Villavicencio, in between making the rounds trying to drum up support for the search team, Manuel had visited a fortune teller. The *vidente*, as they are known in Spanish, have long been a fixture in Colombian culture. Rarely does a radio ad-break go by without a commercial touting love potions or revenge hexes. They are consulted by sports stars, cocaine bosses, and presidents of the republic. In a dark room, a vidente by the name of Jeimy had taken Manuel's hand and made connection with the lost souls in the jungle. The pilot was dead, she told him, but the other passengers had escaped unharmed. The news had bolstered Manuel's resolve and, with the force of character he possessed, Ladino realized it was useless to try to prevent him from joining the search.

Instead, Ladino gave Edwin Paky a set of coordinates. They had been sent through by air force pilots who, during their sweep of the area, had spotted a break in the canopy seven kilometers to the north-west of where the soldiers were searching. It looked big enough to have been caused by a falling plane.

At Cachiporro, the search team haggled for a few rusty machetes, some fariña, and a decrepit outboard motor. As they traveled upriver, it broke down repeatedly, and it took them eight hours to reach Casa Dumar. They arrived exhausted, and slept in the lancha under a tarp to escape the clouds of mosquitoes around the house.

The next day, they set off early, traveling upstream, with two of Dumar's sons joining the search team. On the river, Nestor Andoke took in his surroundings. He was renowned as one of Araracuara's most proficient trackers and hunters, a man who knew the monte better than anyone. To the expert eye, each jungle is different, and he noticed that this was a wilder habitat than his native Caquetá.

"The river was the color of coffee, and it was full of fish with beautiful rapids," he recalls. "It's a virgin monte—there are no communities, it hasn't been exploited."

After half an hour, they docked at the riverside and pulled the lancha up onto the muddy shore. An hour later, they had pushed through the jungle and reached the specified coordinates. They found nothing but a couple of trees blown over by a storm. They craned their necks and looked up at the gray clouds through the gap in the canopy. Then they looked at each other. Delio was disappointed and exhausted, slumped against one of the fallen trees. Manuel stomped around, hacking away at the undergrowth with his machete.

Edwin checked his GPS again. They were in the right spot.

They had a choice to make. Call in their findings and return to Casa Dumar? Or continue the search?

The decision was unanimous.

While the commandos were motivated by a sense of professional duty, reinforced by the confidence that comes from years of training and preparation for jungle warfare, the Indigenous search team was driven forward by something more personal: a desperate search for their loved ones.

Manuel was the dynamo. His certainty that his family was alive was absolute. If any member of the team considered questioning his assumption, one look from Manuel was enough to dissuade them. Manuel explained to the men how, the previous year, his own sister, a deaf mute, had gone missing from Puerto Sábalo. He had searched for her in the monte for a month before she eventually turned up, having survived on a diet of seeds and fruits. The plane carrying his family had crashed only a week ago—they still had time.

They made camp, and came up with a different plan. If Herman had walked away from the crash, as Manuel insisted he knew to be the case, it was logical that he would have led any survivors to the river. The soldiers were searching to the south, so it made sense for them to push on north, along the banks of the Apaporis, in the direction of the El Tigre rapids.

For the next three days, they moved in four teams of three, fanned out across the western bank of the river. The first man hacked the path with a machete; the second took charge of navigation; and the final man carried the bulk of the food and equipment. From the first moments, however, the going was tough. They had to cross streams and swamps, and the often-deafening noise of the water forced them to bunch close together to communicate.

"There were many hills, and it was the rainy season, when the waters rise and all the streams and branches of the river are full," recalls Henry Guerrero. "What made it harder was that the vegetation was so thick, much thicker than we were used to in Caquetá."

Henry was a family friend of Manuel and Magdalena, and the son of a cacique in Araracuara. For a period, he had taught at the school in Puerto Sábalo that Lesly had attended. He remembered her as a shy, quiet girl, but also as an observant and intelligent student. He had grown fond of her, and she, in turn, had called him *tio*, uncle. When the request to assist the search for the family had been relayed to him, he had been instrumental in gathering the team. Now, however, as he looked down at his soaked sneakers, he wondered if they had been too hasty.

The team had arrived with little more than the clothes on their backs, expecting to be provided with the search equipment necessary for a jungle expedition—gumboots, mosquito nets, food—once they arrived in Cachiporro. They were out of luck. And now the foray to the site of the gap in the canopy had turned into a multi-day expedition.

Delio Mendoza lagged behind. He was Herman's younger brother, and he resembled him, except that his features were softer, his body a little rounder, and he didn't have Herman's confident politician's smile. His elbows and knees throbbed with tendonitis, and he popped a painkiller every time the group stopped to take water. "We suffered a lot down there," he told me later. "Every day was an agony." As the rain plastered his shirt to his body and the shrubs tugged at his shins, Delio was alone with his thoughts.

He remembered being six years old, standing in rank with the other students in the cloisters of Araracuara's boarding school, as Herman was brought before them by a Capuchin priest. His elder brother dropped his pants and received several blows of the wooden paddle, as punishment for having stolen mangoes from the priest's personal orchard. Delio remembered the twinge of admiration he had felt at that moment.

His brother had always been one to resist unjust authority. In the 1990s, both boys were among the first Uitoto children to study at university in Bogotá. Herman, gregarious and forceful, was quick to become involved with the nascent Indigenous-rights movements of the time. His career had taken off from there. He became an influential activist, as happy rubbing shoulders with politicians in the capital as organizing assemblies in Amazonian malocas.

Delio had taken a different path. I met him in Leticia, the most developed city in the Colombian Amazon, where he worked at the Sinchi Institute, a national scientific program. It was a comfortable position in air-conditioned offices. He gave the impression of having lived in his brother's shadow, and now, in his fifties, he confessed that he wondered if he was losing touch with the monte, with his Indigenous culture, with the boy he had been.

He'd been nervous when they entered the jungle. He didn't have Manuel's physical fitness, Edwin's navigational skills, or Henry and Nestor's long-nurtured connection to the jungle. But their conviction rubbed off on him, and their experience gave him confidence. "Manuel didn't seem worried—he seemed to know what he was doing, and he was always focused on the search," he remembers. He knew that his brother's life depended on them. It drove him on through the pain in his joints.

He recalled a time, during the wet season when the rivers ran clear, that he and Herman had stolen a canoe and stared down together at the fish swimming beneath them. "When I remembered these things, I felt the urge to return to those moments, to fish, to walk in the monte, to explore," he says. "Perhaps that's the whole idea of being an Indigenous, to search for whatever there is to find." The jungle had seemed so familiar then. He realized that a life spent in Bogotá and Leticia had dulled his instincts, had made him forget what had once come naturally. As he followed the trail beaten through the shrub by his more experienced companions, Delio tried to locate the spirit of that child in his weary fifty-year-old frame.

That first night, after they changed into their dry clothes and rolled out their tarps on the ground, the men dipped into the fariña supplies and discussed the territory they had walked. They compared it to the tales their grandfathers had told about the place. For the People of the Center, the jungles to the north of Caquetá had an ominous reputation. The rapids of the Apaporis were said to devour anyone that tried to pass them, while the calmer stretches were home to man-eating boas. Jaguars slunk along the branches of the trees.

They tribes that inhabited this dark and barren jungle were also a source of fascination. Their culture was very different from that of the People of the Center. They worshiped a hero known as Yuruparí, and their powerful shamans regularly imbibed *yagé*, the juice from a hallucinogenic vine, to converse with the guardian spirits of the jungle. Historically, they had been enemies of the People of the Center.

"In the old times, the Uitoto had many confrontations with these peoples," says Manuel. "We respect their culture, of course, but they worship other gods. They know how to turn themselves into jaguars and boas."

Even the tribes that inhabited the lower reaches of the

Apaporis retained an ancestral fear of the people who populated the headwaters. The Makuna tribe of the lower Apaporis believe that the river's spectacular rapids and gorges were created by the jungle spirits at the behest of an ancient shaman to protect them from cannibal raiders who lived upriver.

The late-night discussion did little to calm their nerves. Throughout the night, the noises of the jungle—distant howls, the creaking of branches, rustling in the undergrowth—took on more ominous qualities. Shortly after daybreak, Edwin Paky was awoken by a thump on his leg. Lifting his head, he found himself staring at the eyes and flickering tongue of a six-foot snake, stunned and dangerous, having fallen from the branches above. He waited, still as a stone, until the unexpected visitor regained its senses and slithered off into the undergrowth.

That morning and every morning after, Manuel was up first. As his companions put on their wet clothes from the previous day and chewed on some cold, damp casabe, it was his voice, in turns encouraging and hectoring, that formed the backdrop to their preparations.

On May 13, they reached a bend in the river where small pockets of white water rippled over the rocks that lay deep on the riverbed. In the dry season, the El Tigre rapids were another of the Apaporis's famously impassible obstacles, but now the river was high and wide, engorged by the constant downpours.

Edwin checked his GPS, removed his baseball cap, and flicked the sweat from his hair. Henry took off his sneakers and poured the murky water they contained onto the ground. In their knapsacks, they hunted for the few hotdog sausages and handfuls of fariña that remained. The rapids marked the logical boundary of their search area, an impassible point which any survivors from the crash were unlikely to have pushed beyond. There was nowhere left to search. They had reached a dead end. They strung up their hammocks in silence, in desperate need of a clue.

That night, Edwin had a dream. He was on a lancha in the fast-moving waters of El Tigre, the outboard motor spluttering and coughing against the current. The white water pushed his boat back and spun it around until, exhausted, he entered an eddy and supported the boat against a rock.

As he rested, he saw, on the shore, a house on a hill. The surrounding slopes were full of people dressed in white, eating, drinking, and laughing. From the crowd of revelers, a beautiful young girl in a blue dress emerged. Edwin intuited that it was her *quinciñera*, the traditional coming-of-age party for girls of fifteen. She smiled at him and beckoned him, and, as he started to walk towards her over the grassy riverside, he looked back to see that the lancha had drifted off downstream with the current.

"That's a good dream," Nestor Andoke told him the next morning over breakfast. "Whenever you have a dream like that, it means the search is going well."

The People of the Center place great faith in the power and meaning of dreams. In Nestor's opinion, one which was shared by all, it meant that the children were still alive. There was no turning back now—they would find the plane and its passengers.

Edwin's premonitions aside, it wasn't immediately obvious in what way the search was going well. They were miles upstream from where the army was searching, and they had no way of getting back easily.

They spent that morning fishing, pulling in a heartening haul of a dozen *palometas*, a narrow-bodied fish related to the piranha, but without its cousin's fearsome jaws. As they cooked their lunch over the fire, they heard a lancha approaching.

"I'm not bringing supplies," a voice shouted from on board.

"I'm bringing new information."

It was Andrés Londoño. The leader of the Avianline rescue team had returned to help the search. The previous day, he had landed at Casa Dumar by helicopter, accompanied by a team of firemen. The latter had taken one look at the dense forest and the pouring rain, and had flown out the next day. But that afternoon, Dumar had given up his secret.

He had taken Londoño out to the coca plantation, and shown him where he had seen the Cessna flying close to the treetops on the morning of May 1. Londoño had traced the trajectory of its flight, and realized it led to the same area he had searched on his first day in the jungle. Furthermore, he had on his phone a video that had been sent to him by one of the Cessna pilots who had made the initial flyovers. In the background, a steady beeping could be heard, which increased in frequency until it was almost a single high note. It was the sound of the ELT beacon. The pilot had been flying right over the location of the Cessna.

The men huddled around the phone for an hour, studying the curves in the river visible from the cockpit, and comparing them to their maps of the Apaporis. They reached the same conclusion: they had been searching an area miles away from where the plane had crashed.

Edwin felt anger welling up. He could have wrung Fredy Ladino's neck at that moment. It seemed to him that the Indigenous search team were being handled with kid gloves by Avianline and the military. On the face of it, they had been encouraged to participate, but had been sent off to an area where they couldn't interfere with the real search. They were braving hunger, the rains, and the mosquitoes on a wild goose chase.

Edwin sent a message back to Avianline, using Londoño's GPS. "I got mad, and I told Fredy to send us to the real search site," remembers Edwin. "No matter the soldiers, the guerrillas, or whatever else, that's where we were going."

On the lancha back to Casa Dumar, the men made a pact. When they found the plane, they would not tell the soldiers. They would announce it themselves. The military were not to be trusted. As the spray from the prow glowed gold in the setting sun, Edwin Paky thought again of the girl in the blue dress.

CHAPTER TWELVE

Milpesos

The day they left the banks of the Apaporis behind, the children didn't eat. Under sheets of rain, they walked without a destination, their soaked clothes weighing them down. Lesly went first. Behind, her younger siblings tried to step in the footprints she made. At the back, Tien kept stopping to try to kick free the clumps of mud that encased his sneakers. They zigzagged and circled as Lesly kept her eyes out for any signs of a footpath. Outside of La Chorrera and Puerto Sábalo, one couldn't walk too far in the jungle before coming across a muddy track that led to a village, but now she saw nothing but decaying leaves.

When darkness came, Soleiny cradled Cristin, and Tien held the flashlight to illuminate Lesly's work as she hacked at palm leaves with the scissors. The thick, fibrous stems resisted their blunt edges, but she persevered. When she was done, she took the four leaves and wove their fronds together to create single covering. She propped it against a tree, laid the towel on the dirty floor, and the children crawled underneath.

The next day, Lesly spotted the white bark of a familiar tree. Her eyes racing up along its trunk, she saw the huge fronds that funneled upwards like a cone, and at the base of the leaves, two large bunches of black fibers that hung like shaggy manes of braided hair. It was the milpeso palm. In among the fibers, Lesly could see the tree's dark-purple fruits. The skins glistened with the moisture of the jungle.

The milpeso palm was one of the most cherished trees in the Uitoto world. They took many years to reach maturity, but they had a multitude of uses. The leaves were the preferred roofing materials for the maloca. When cut down, the trunks served as the perfect breeding ground for *mojojoy*, the jungle grubs that were delicious when fried and salted. The brown flesh of the fruit was hard, but it could be softened in warm water. Lesly remembered her mother with her hands in a bowl of water, squeezing the fruit until it broke away from the seed, massaging the mixture between her fingers until it turned into a soup the color of milky tea. The juice was full of energy and protein; some mothers gave it to their babies as a substitute for milk.

The children knelt around the base of the palm and brushed away the leaves with their hands, collecting handfuls of purple fruit. Lesly knew another way to eat them: if you kept the fruit in your mouth long enough, the heat and moisture would eventually break down the flesh. She gave one piece of fruit each to Soleiny and Tien to suck on, and put two in her own mouth. Then she stashed the remaining fruit in her backpack. When she felt the first fruit begin to soften, she added some water, squashed it in the palm of her hand, and fed it to Cristin. The baby sucked it happily from her fingers.

Lesly opened the backpack and looked at the dozen or so milpeso fruits inside. She wondered how long they would last. How long they would need to last.

The following day, as the children traced the banks of a stream upriver, Tien made a face. He asked what the smell was. Lesly inhaled the familiar, nauseating odor. It was the same one she had smelled on the day they had left the plane. It brought back the image of her mother, her hair hanging down, the awkward angles of her body.

Ahead, through the dense foliage, she saw a gleam of white paint. Without meaning to, the children had returned to the wreck of HK-2803.

Ahead lay the vultures, the flies, and her mother's dead body, but Lesly knew she had to return. Maybe someone had found the plane. Maybe they were waiting for them there. At the very least, she could replace the clothes that were already falling to pieces on the children's bodies.

While Tien and Soleiny waited with Cristin, Lesly crept cautiously towards the plane. There were more vultures now. They fanned their wings, perched on the fuselage. They bickered and lurched at each other on the forest floor. She kept to the right-hand side of the plane, away from her mother's body. The area around the plane was just as she had left it. There was no sign that anybody had been there.

At the point where she had established the shelter on the first night, she found her mother's bag. She opened it, took out new changes of clothes for each of the children, and collected them in a bundle. As she was preparing to head back to where her siblings were waiting, she glanced again at the plane. In the shade of the left-hand wing, she noticed something. It was a black strap.

Holding her breath, she approached the plane and tugged at the strap. It was Herman Mendoza's backpack. She retreated a few yards and unzipped the bag. Under the clothes and wash kit, she found a tin of tuna and a plastic bag full of a yellow grain: fariña. She smashed the can repeatedly against a thick protruding root. She managed to dent it, but it wouldn't break. She threw the can on the floor in frustration.

As the children changed into the fresh clothes, Lesly noticed that their arms and legs were covered in red insect bites. On Soleiny's left wrist there were angry red nodules, which she recognized as the early signs of leishmaniasis. She knew they would soon burst open and form ulcers, and that the open wound would start to grow. She took a strap of gauze and wrapped it around her sister's wrist.

Cristin was also sick. She had a blocked nose and was breathing through her mouth. Her forehead was hot to the touch. She had the flu, thought Lesly, and she prayed that the baby did not develop a fever. Lesly poured some water into the baby's bottle and mixed in a small handful of fariña. She swirled the bottle until it produced a cream-colored mixture, and coaxed the teat between Cristin's lips.

Lesly sensed that time was running out. The fariña could keep them going a little longer, but she was worried about sickness. She needed to find a place where her sisters could get treatment. She had tried waiting by the plane, but a week after the crash no one had come for them, and she wondered if they were searching for her at all. She had tried going to the riverbanks, but they were deserted.

The only option seemed to be to head west. As they went, they found a juan soco tree. At its base, in the leaves, lay a round, yellow fruit. Lesly burst open the skin and sucked on the sweet flesh. As she passed the fruit to Tien, the children heard aircraft overhead. But when they looked up, all they could see was the perfect green dome of the canopy.

CHAPTER THIRTEEN

The Wreckage

Captain Edwin Montiel squatted next to the radio. For eight days, he had provided the same sorry report to the combined operations base in San José del Guaviare. *Clear. Clear. Clear.*

They had found nothing. No sign of the aircraft. No signs of survivors. When the rains stopped, the jungle had been eerily silent. It was a relief, one day, when a family of Humboldt monkeys hurled feces at them from the treetops. This was, at least, a sign of life.

The only report of note had come from the Ares 3 team on the third day of the search. They had come across an area where the trees had been bent back to form a clearing. On the ground were some old black tarps, traces of food, and two shirts bearing the EMC's insignia. It was a guerrilla camp, but, judging by the state of decay, the commandos concluded that it had been abandoned at least a year previously. Other than that, there were no traces of its former occupants—not a single footprint.

The discovery seemed to confirm that the guerrillas were long gone. The threat of ambush receded, and the commandos changed their tactics. The started to work in teams of two instead of four, halving the time it took to clear each square on the search grid. Now, however, they were running out of squares to search. Each man had walked over 150 kilometers, and now Dragon 4 were bumping up against areas already cleared by Destroyer 1 and Ares 3.

It didn't make sense. How was it possible that three teams of commandos had spent a week meticulously searching the area around the ELT signal and had not found the plane? They began to doubt their technology, their orders, their own capability. They began to look for other explanations.

Was it possible that the ELT had fallen from the plane some time before it crashed? Had the pilot made it to the river after all, and were the remains of the Cessna now lying on the bed of the Apaporis? Was it all a hoax? Had the flight been hijacked by a passenger to make a cocaine shipment to a remote jungle airstrip?

That night, as he lay in his hammock with the din of mosquitoes brushing up against his net, Montiel couldn't sleep. He had a sense of impending failure, but also, as a man who prided himself on his planning and strategy, a relentless curiosity.

"We had highly trained people with every communication system, the latest technology, a huge back-up staff," says Montiel. "But, despite all this, I was still asking myself, *What happened to the plane?*"

The next morning was May 15. Morale was low. At 6.00am, the soldiers packed up their kits and began to march. Sergeant Wilmer Miranda led the men out in single file.

Four hundred meters away from their camp, his tracker's eyes noticed something: a number of branches were bent back, and others lay snapped on the leafy floor, as if disturbed by a passing animal. He held up a sweaty palm. The troops stopped.

Miranda moved forward, stepping soundlessly through the

undergrowth. Twenty meters further on, he saw a small, bright-pink object on the ground ahead of him. He crouched and listened, scanning the thick foliage for any sign of an ambush. Then he approached.

It was a baby's bottle, hourglass-shaped, with two pink handles and a teat. His companions, hastening through the jungle to join him, could barely contain their excitement.

"It was an emotional moment," he remembers, "because up until then we'd found nothing. We didn't have a single clue—we'd spent nine days with no information."

The bottle was half-full of murky water, and there was sediment at the bottom. It had been filled from a stream. The bottle hadn't been thrown from the plane; it had been used, right there on the jungle floor. Montiel took a photo of the bottle and sent it to operations headquarters so that it could be identified by relatives as belonging to the children who'd been aboard HK-2803. But Montiel already knew in his gut that it belonged to the children.

Two hundred meters further on, his suspicion was confirmed. On the ground were the remains of a broken-into juan soco fruit. On its yellow husk were the indentations of small teeth. They were not animal marks, they concluded, but human—a child's. That morning, they had suspected their search would be in vain; now, they were filled with a new energy and urgency.

"The day we found the baby bottle was a great day that filled us with hope," Montiel recalls. "The majority of my team, we're fathers, we're husbands. In one way or another, that motivated us in the search." The children had made it out of the plane.

But if the bottle provided an answer of sorts, the soldiers of Dragon 4 didn't have long to ruminate on its meaning. By that same afternoon, a whole series of new questions would emerge.

* * *

Later that morning, Edwin Paky was swinging in a hammock at Casa Dumar. The owner had lent it to him the previous night, and after five nights of sleeping on the forest floor, it had been a blessing. Now, however, the air was thick with mosquitoes. A few had managed to slip under the net and were nipping at his ankles.

"I started thinking, *It's only 10.00am. What the hell am I going to do lying here the whole day? I came here to search*," he recalls. He looked over to where Nestor was swatting the bugs away from his head. Edwin walked over to him.

"Screw this, let's get out of here," he said.

Nestor and the other four men from Araracuara agreed to join Edwin. So, too, did a sixteen-year-old boy from Cachiporro named Alejandro. Manuel and Delio stayed behind. They planned to head back to Cachiporro the following day to update their relatives and to source more supplies.

Edwin was convinced the plane had crashed south of Casa Dumar. Londoño's account of the first day's search, Dumar's belated eye-witness report of the low-flying Cessna, the beeps of the ELT on the pilot's video—all the evidence pointed towards this conclusion.

They set off again into the jungle, and shortly after 2.00pm they heard the sound of a chainsaw. A group of soldiers was cutting back trees to create a clearing for the heliport. Edwin approached the army captain, who appeared to be in charge of the operation. He knew the soldiers would try to discourage him from entering the search area, but his mind was made up, and he didn't mince his words.

"We're going in," he told the captain. "Nobody is going to get rid of us until we find our friend."

The soldier was in a spot. He could tell from Edwin's expression that he wouldn't be deterred, but he was under orders not to let civilians into the search area. He decided to point Edwin and his team to an area a couple of kilometers north-west of the heliport. It was among the grids that the army had already searched, so the civilians would be unlikely to cross paths with the commandos.

The men set off at a pace. They came across a trail broken by the Avianline search team, and covered the distance in an hour. Now they knew they were searching in the right place, they felt a surge of energy, a renewed sense of purpose. But, once again, time was not on their side.

By 5.00pm they had found nothing. The men had little appetite for another night in hammocks in the rain, not when Casa Dumar was five kilometers away. Edwin took a bearing back to the house, and the men spread out, using their machetes once again to beat a direct path back. The thought of the tin roof and fried fish and rice cooked by Dumar's wife spurred them on. They heard a shout.

"Look! A blue house!"

It came from Alejandro, the boy from Cachiporro. Edwin rushed forward. "It's the plane," he said.

The Cessna was in a vertical position, its blue belly facing them. Alejandro had mistaken the plane for a dwelling. Edwin moved swiftly to check the numbers painted on the tail: HK-2803.

"I felt as if my body was lifted from the ground," remembers Edwin. "There had been days of expectation, doubt, and worry, but at last we had completed our mission."

As he got closer, however, he felt a knot in his stomach. Vultures spread their wings and flew away as he approached. A thick swarm of flies buzzed around the body of the plane. The nose of the Cessna was buried so deeply that the cockpit was barely visible above the ground.

"The moment I saw that, I thought no one could have survived," he remembers. "For me, they were all dead."

In the fading light, he moved to the left-hand side of the aircraft. He saw a woman's dark hair hanging down. Her badly decomposed body was slumped forward; the back of her seat had been pushed forward. Beneath her, he could make out the pilot's white shirt against the dark forest floor. The other side of the aircraft had taken even more serious damage. But in the growing darkness he couldn't make out Herman's body.

The other members of the Indigenous search team had joined Edwin at the site. As they peered around the surrounding area, they shared a growing realization. What had looked like debris thrown clear in the crash had an order to it. A white shirt was hanging from a branch. A diaper bag was open, with its contents removed. A tin of sardines was dented from multiple impacts, and two bottles of water lay next to it. The children had survived. Edwin hoped Herman was with them, somewhere in the jungle.

The men huddled together. Still indignant about the way they had been diverted from the real search site, still distrustful of the soldiers, they remembered their pact to announce the discovery themselves, lest the military find a way to steal their credit. Now, however, the logistical challenges associated with this plan became apparent. They lacked the body bags, gloves, and facemasks needed to evacuate the bodies to the river, which, from GPS readings, was still four kilometers away. It would take four hours to hack their way through with machetes and it was already dark.

In the end, they decided to retrace their steps to the heliport, where they notified the soldiers. At Casa Dumar, Manuel and Delio were waiting for them. Over a meal of fried fish, they told them what they had seen. They were unsure if Delio's brother was alive or dead, they said, but it seemed that the children had survived the crash.

The next morning, Edwin Montiel's Destroyer 4 team hastened towards the crash site, approximately 3.5 kilometers to the east of where they had found the baby's bottle. En route, they made another discovery: a simple shelter made from several large palm fronds stacked together. To the side lay a pair of children's scissors, with rounded tips and purple handles.

The soldiers investigated the stems of the palms, which appeared to have been cut with the scissors and were still relatively fresh. They estimated that whoever had built the shelter had done so five days previously. They took photos, and radioed the information back to headquarters before continuing.

As they reached their destination, there were no signs that they were approaching a crash site. "We always thought that we'd find fallen trees all around, or that there would be a smell," says Montiel, "But when the GPS said we were fifty meters from the wreckage, we still couldn't see the plane, and there was no bad smell. We got closer—thirty meters, twenty, fifteen—and then, when we were ten meters away, we saw the plane. It was totally perpendicular … it was hoisted up like a flag. That's why the air force aircraft couldn't find it when they passed overhead—it was completely hidden by the tall trees."

Following their combat training, Ares 3 team provided a defensive cordon around the area, in case of ambush. Montiel's team set about clearing the undergrowth around the plane. Rigging up a set of ropes and pulleys over the branches of the trees, they were able to hoist the plane by its tail. Underneath the pilot's side of the craft, they confirmed, was the body of Captain Hernando Murcia. They also found the remains of Herman Mendoza. His body had been crushed into the ground. His head lay several feet away, under the debris of the plane.

At Casa Dumar, the Indigenous heard the grim news over the radio. They turned to look at Delio. He sat motionless, staring at the ground.

"I'd always hoped that we'd find Herman alive," Delio told me, three months later. "All of my prayers were that he had found something to eat, that he could walk and get to some safe point. When I received the news, it was painful, of course, and I thought of the possible suffering he went through, his last words. It was sad the way they found him, with his head separated from his body, with the worms."

That morning, the men gathered round Delio. They hugged him and gave him ambil to fortify his journey to the crash site. When he saw what remained of his brother, he sunk to his knees and hung his head, softly repeating, "*Hermanito*", which means "little Herman", as well as "little brother."

Manuel, too, was distraught. He had been driven on by the fortune teller's conviction that his family had survived the crash. Now he was shocked to find Magdalena's body, slumped forward in its seat, little more than hair and bones.

When he remembers this moment, his voice cracks and his eyes fill with tears.

"I felt terrible," he says. "I'd always believed, up to that moment, that they were all still alive."

Manuel's plan to help Magdalena and the children escape

from the jungle had ended in tragedy. His girlfriend, the mother of his two children, was dead. When he turned away from the plane, breathing heavily, trying to keep his emotions in check, something caught his eye. In among the leaves of the forest floor was the husk of a copuazú fruit. He buried his grief, he says, with a new sense of purpose.

"I saw the traces of where they had slept, of where they had eaten," he recalls. "Up ahead, the soldiers had found the baby's bottle. That gave us strength, it fueled us, it gave us remedy. We had found the plane—now we had to find the children."

They couldn't have gone far, the Indigenous searchers agreed, and that afternoon Manuel's prayers were answered. At 3.30pm, word came through on the radio that the children had been found. An Avianline pilot had arrived with supplies at Cachiporro, where a group of locals told him the children had been spotted on a lancha, traveling downriver. They would arrive at Cachiporro before 5.00pm.

The soldiers tried to confirm the sighting, but the news traveled fast. The OPIAC, the Indigenous rights organization that Herman Mendoza belonged to, announced it on their radio show.

"Today we can confirm that the children were found by the Indigenous search team," one of its directors said. Then, in a sign of the animosity generated by the handling of search, he continued: "The Indigenous team has achieved a great task. However, media groups and some institutions want to cover up [their] work."

At 4.43pm, President Gustavo Petro took to X and posted to his seven million followers.

"After the arduous search work of our Armed Forces, we have found the four children who disappeared in the airplane accident in Guaviare alive. It's a joy for the country," he said.

But it was not the end. It was barely the beginning. Five o'clock came and went with no sign of the children. The night grew thick over the jungle and the hopes of the rescue team.

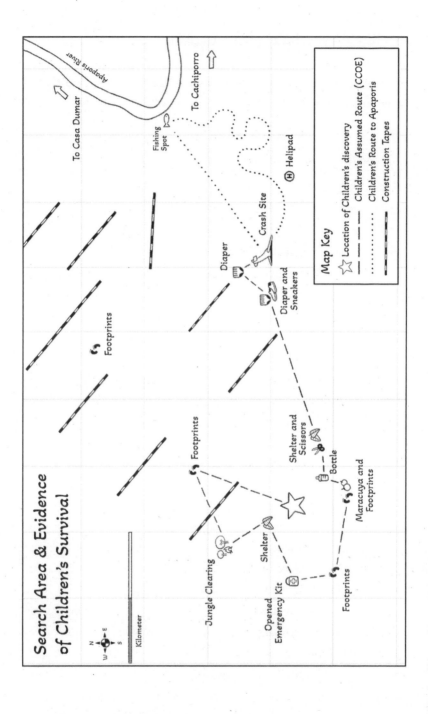

Search Area & Evidence of Children's Survival

Apaporis River

To Casa Dumar

To Cachiporro

Fishing Spot

Diaper

Diaper and Sneakers

Crash Site

Ⓗ Helipad

Footprints

Footprints

Shelter and Scissors

Bottle

Maracuya and Footprints

Jungle Clearing

Shelter

Opened Emergency Kit

Footprints

Kilometer

N W E S

Map Key

☆ Location of Children's discovery

— Children's Assumed Route (CCOE)

--- Children's Route to Apaporis

⋯ Construction Tapes

CHAPTER FOURTEEN

The Vortex

The jungle swallowed them up.

Until the emergence of Gabriel García Márquez, the closing words of Eustacio Rivera's 1924 novel, *The Vortex*, were the most famous in Colombian literature. The novel purports to be the diary of a young urban poet as he ventures into the Amazon in search of a lost lover. Soon, however, he finds himself disorientated by a "ceaseless monotony of green." In this "emerald prison," his mind begins to unravel, and the mark of insanity creeps into his writing, like a virulent jungle fungus.

Although Rivera had intended *The Vortex* as a critique of the rubber trade, it was his terrifying, florid descriptions of the jungle that lingered longest in the memory for generations of Colombians who studied the book at school. For the vast majority of people who lived in the Andean valleys or along the Caribbean coast, the book cemented the idea of the country's southern jungle as a green hell, a place uniquely hostile to the physical and mental integrity of anyone who ventured in too deep.

So when the wreckage of HK-2803 was found and details of the various clues that suggested the children had survived became public, local journalists dusted off their copies of *The Vortex* for inspiration. "Did the Jungle Swallow Them Up?" ran one headline.

The reports of the children's rescue had proven untrue. The morning after announcing the news, President Petro deleted his post. Local and international media groups hastily spiked their web stories.

The source of the misinformation was never identified. According to Fredy Ladino, the inhabitants of Cachiporro had heard, over shortwave radio, that the children had been spotted in a lancha. When they relayed this information to an Avianline pilot and he, in turn, updated the company, a soldier present in the operations room had leaked it to the press. Who was responsible for the original radio broadcast? Was it a simple error or a prank? These questions were never answered, and they were soon forgotten as the mystery of the children's disappearance captivated the country.

Two weeks had passed since the Cessna had disappeared, and few Colombians held any hope of finding survivors. The country has a rotten history of air disasters. In addition to the fallen airmen recognized at Villavicencio airport, there have been countless high-profile cases. In 1989, a Boeing 727 was blown up on the orders of Pablo Escobar. Six years later, a 757 crashed into a mountain outside the city of Cali. In 2016, a charter flight ran out of fuel and crashed into the forests around Medellín, taking with it an entire Brazilian soccer team. But, suddenly, in the case of the missing Cessna, there seemed to be hope of a happy ending.

It was now the biggest story of the year. Colombians tuned in to the news hoping for updates or new clues as to the children's whereabouts. Online sleuths proposed theories about the children's fate. The military's operations base in San José del Guaviare was inundated with calls from psychics instructing them where to search next. International news crews started to increase their coverage.

The pressure was building on General Pedro Sánchez. The children's relatives were angry that their hopes had been raised and dashed by the false alarm. They released a press statement condemning the misinformation and reminding the media that their "physical and emotional health is not a game." Meanwhile, Indigenous groups were incensed that credit for discovering the plane had been given to the military. President Petro, embarrassed by his premature and ill-advised post, needed a successful resolution to the search more than ever.

Finding the plane had been tough enough. Locating four children wandering the forest would be exponentially harder. A new, more intense stage of the search had begun. Sánchez called it Operation Hope.

"We had to send in more troops," says Sánchez. "For me, these were the golden hours. I thought we had, at a maximum, five days to find them."

On May 18, three more commando teams were dropped into the jungle, and more teams were mobilized to join them. By early June, the Intermediate Operations Post at Calamar would find itself supplying sixteen teams, its Huey helicopter working round the clock to rappel dehydrated food, cooking-gas cannisters, and insect repellent to the troops below. The search area was widened to seventeen kilometers by nineteen kilometers to take into account that the children might have wandered beyond the initial radius.

In addition to more manpower, a new approach was needed. Edwin Paky's team had discovered the plane in a quadrant previously cleared by the soldiers. Given the thickness of the vegetation and the limited visibility, the X-shape patrol pattern employed by the soldiers evidently wasn't effective. There was far too much terrain in the center of the quadrant that escaped their eyeballs.

A new zigzag pattern was introduced. The soldiers now snaked back and forth across each quadrant, leaving only twenty meters between each path. This meant that each soldier now had to walk twelve kilometers, and raised the search time for each quadrant from three hours to fourteen hours. Now a team of commandos could only clear one square kilometer per day, and it meant patrolling into the night, using night-vision goggles. All pretense of stealth was abandoned. Now the soldiers shouted Lesly's name.

In the skies above, the air force dropped hundreds of food kits containing snacks and rehydration fluids. Ten thousand fliers telling the children to stay in place fluttered down through the trees. The Huey helicopter was kitted out with a huge round loudspeaker that pointed out of its open bay doors. As they circled above the jungle, it broadcast a deafening appeal from the children's grandmother addressed to Lesly, telling her to stay in place, that the soldiers were looking for her.

At the operations base in San José del Guaviare, the one hundred-strong support team of intelligence analysts, navigators, and logistics specialists were working sixteen-hour days. They had abandoned their military fatigues for civilian clothes, and they looked tired and drawn. Messy plates and cans of drink sat around on the tables. They looked like students cramming for their final exams.

On May 20, the base received an unexpected visitor. Short and barrel-chested, he wore a loose-fitting white shirt embroidered with geometric designs around the collar and a round hat with a wide brim woven from palm leaves. As news of his arrival spread through the corridors, the support staff gave each other knowing looks. This was going to be awkward.

Giovani Yule had a formidable reputation. He was a member of the Nasa people in Colombia's southern Andes, where the state and Indigenous groups had been in conflict for generations. Now fifty-five, he had made a name for himself organizing strikes, marches, and protests against the state. He was also a close ally of President Petro, who had welcomed him into his new government to lead efforts to return lands to Colombians displaced by violence. He was uncompromising and pugnacious, and he made no secret of his dislike of the armed forces.

"Historically, whenever Indigenous people have fought for their rights, the ones we faced off against were the security forces," he explained to me later. "In the protests, they were the ones who hit us and gassed us. The security forces killed many of my companions. When I stepped into [the army base], it was with deep mistrust."

Yule arrived, accompanied by a dozen members of the Indigenous Guard. General Sánchez welcomed them, shook each man's hand, and led them into the operations room. On the wall hung a large map, almost totally green except for the blue curls of the River Apaporis on the upper-right-hand corner. Photos of the baby's bottle, the children's footprints, and the chewed fruit were pinned to the locations where they had been found. Dozens of small red squares marked where the troops had spent the night. On the grid, quadrants that had been searched were struck through with diagonal black lines. These squares now stretched eight kilometers to the west and south-west of where the plane had crashed.

Sánchez offered Yule a coffee. Yule asked for a water, and got straight to the point. He had come on orders from the president's office. He was there to secure the entrance of new Indigenous search teams into the jungle.

General Sánchez was in an awkward position. An old-school Colombian general would have seen the arrival, and its presidential blessing, as undermining his operational authority. The armed forces had traditionally taken a very dim view of the legality and practices of the Indigenous Guard security forces that Yule represented. Two months previously, members of the Colombian security forces had been incensed by the brutal murder of a policeman in Caquetá. The perpetrators were members of the Campesino Guard, a sister organization made up of non-Indigenous members of the rural working class. To his critics, it was evidence that Petro's political attacks on the armed forces had undermined the military's authority, jeopardized the security situation in the countryside, and emboldened those who would commit such a shocking act of indiscriminate vigilantism. If Sánchez didn't share that opinion, he knew that many of his colleagues did, and he was keenly aware of the optics.

"I thought to myself, *If a soldier, active or retired, saw me now, he'd think I was an Indigenous, receiving the killers of policemen*," he says. "But I decided to give him all the information we had, in order to build trust, so they could see we were doing things right."

He updated Yule and his men on the new measures being implemented under Operation Hope. But when it came to Yule's demands, the general knew he had to tread carefully. The Indigenous search teams had already proved their worth on the ground, but the introduction of dozens of new civilians could jeopardize the operational integrity of the mission and put lives at risk.

"I told them, the most important thing is that we search for the children, but the next is that we make it clear who is who. We are the legitimate force of the state, and we have a monopoly on weapons," he remembers saying. "But we also know that you have a great knowledge, and that you're here to help, and that it will be easier to find them if we unite and work together."

He had hit the right tone. Yule seemed to find the terms reasonable. To finish off, Sánchez told him a bit of his own story. He was from a humble background, the son of a bricklayer and a schoolteacher in a small town north of Bogotá, and he'd risen in the stuffy, elitist world of the Colombian military on his own merits. What's more, he too had Indigenous blood. His grandparents had belonged to the Guane tribe, a people all but destroyed during the Spanish conquest.

Yule got up from his chair and crossed the room. He opened his arms wide and embraced Sánchez.

"This is the first time in my life I hug a general from the Colombian army," he whispered in his ear.

That simple gesture, a hug, marked the beginning of a new spirit of cooperation and respect between the army and the Indigenous teams, without which the children might never have been found.

In the coming weeks, the search for Lesly and her siblings took on a decidedly Indigenous flavor. Yule sent out messages to his network of Indigenous peoples across the country. He called on them to perform a "spiritual *minga*."

In Indigenous communities, a minga is a process by which different clans and groups gather to achieve a common goal. Fields are cleared and houses are built through mingas. Protests are organized. On this occasion, Yule called upon on the country's diverse Indigenous groups to go to their sacred sites and perform their own rituals, to ask their spirits and mother nature to return the children safely.

In the days that followed, he received videos and messages of rituals performed by the Wayuu people of the northern deserts, the Kogi people of the snowcapped mountains, and many tribes across the Amazon.

"They called me to say they had opened a spiritual path for us to travel safely," he says. "They told us that the children were still alive, that they were weak, but that we would find them."

On May 21, fifty men formed a semicircle on the grass outside the army base, facing south towards the jungle. They were soldiers and Indigenous—Yule and Sánchez among them—and they stood with their arms over each other's shoulders. Yule led a ritual, requesting the spirits of the jungle to grant them safe passage. Then the Indigenous reinforcements boarded the Black Hawk that stood on the tarmac.

After they had gone, Sánchez stepped out of the gates of the army base into a forest of microphones and a storm of questions. Were the children still alive? How could Colombia's finest soldiers fail to find four children in the jungle? What were his thoughts on the inclusion of the new Indigenous searchers?

Sánchez responded with calm authority. The children were still alive, he said.

The grim truth was that the sniffer dogs, which had already been in the search area for several days, would have easily tracked down their corpses if they were dead. The problem was that the children were moving, and possibly hiding from the rescuers.

"This isn't a search for a needle in a haystack. It's a tiny flea in a vast carpet, because they keep moving," he said.

The reporters began to press him. The general said that the children would be found in a matter of days. The search was now at the three-week mark. As he began to explain the complexities of the terrain and the climate, Sánchez's voice seemed to get caught in his throat. It only lasted a second. He swallowed, blinked, and continued his comments. But no one could mistake the crack of emotion from the stoic soldier. A year later, I asked him what he'd felt at that moment.

"Impotence," he replied. "Impotence and a terrible pain."

CHAPTER FIFTEEN

Flier

"Grandmother Fatima, you understand me. You must stay ..."

The children looked around wildly. The voice of their grandmother seemed to creep up through the trees, surge suddenly past them like wind, and then slip away into the distance, replaced by a rhythmic humming.

Soleiny and Tien looked around, and then looked at their sister for explanation. Lesly had none, but she set off in the direction of the sound. The pain in her leg was beginning to subside, and she moved quicker now, even as her soaked socks slipped in the mud.

"... looking for you ... Lesly. This is your grandmother Fatima, you ..."

This time, their grandmother's voice seemed to sweep across in front of them, disappearing into the forest to the right. Lesly changed her course and began to tramp through the undergrowth, the ferns and branches catching in her jeans. But then the voice would appear behind them.

"Was that Grandma?" asked Soleiny. Lesly didn't know what to tell her.

In the last week, the monte had become more mysterious. The children were disoriented, wandering in circles, trying to find signs of human life.

They were beginning to lose the items they most needed. First, Tien kicked off his muddy sneakers and was determined to carry on in his socks, like Lesly, but his feet had become bruised and blistered. With the scissors, Lesly had cut strips of material from the clothing she carried with her and tied them around his feet like bandages. But then the scissors had gone missing, along with one of the plastic water bottles. When nighttime came, Lesly had to pull and twist the palm leaves, finally biting into the fibrous stems with her teeth to separate them from the tree.

One night, as she prepared to mix the last of the fariña with water for Cristin, Soleiny confessed that she had left the baby's bottle somewhere in the forest. For the first time since the accident, Lesly lost her temper with Soleiny. How was she to feed Cristin without the bottle? She looked around and picked up a wide, round leaf. She bent it at the edges to form a crucible, into which she mixed some fariña and water. Carefully, she poured it from the edge of the leaf into Cristin's mouth.

As the children rested by a fallen tree, they heard men's voices. They were calling Lesly's name. As they approached, she could make out the green uniforms, the rifles over their shoulders. Suddenly fearful, Lesly grabbed Tien and Soleiny by their arms and pulled them under the tree trunk. The men moved closer, until the sound of her own name being called drowned out all other sounds in the jungle. They came within ten meters of the tree trunk. Lesly cupped her hand over Cristin's mouth to keep her from calling out.

A few days later, on May 30, Lesly brought the children to a small clearing. On the ground, she saw a bright red piece of paper. She picked it up, and read the words, written in Spanish and in her native tongue:

We are looking for you
Don't move any more, stay close
to a river or a stream
Make noise
Make smoke
We are going to save you. We are
close. Your grandmother Fatima and the
family are looking for you

Lesly took the mosquito net from her backpack and strung it from a tree. The children got inside. They waited.

CHAPTER SIXTEEN

An Unlikely Alliance

Juan Felipe Montoya was from army stock. His father was in the Colombian army, just like his father before him. He grew up surrounded by men in uniform, absorbing their deep sense of duty to their country, and he never considered any other career. He joined the military academy at the age of sixteen, and after only two years of his active service, his senior officers were convinced he had what it took to be a Special Forces officer.

When I met him in August 2023, in a small apartment on an army base in northern Bogotá, he was just back from another mission, the location and details of which he was unable to disclose. The living room was cluttered with toys. One wall was marked at knee height by felt-tip pens, the work of his two-year-old daughter. From the next room came the occasional wail of a newborn.

With his strong jaw, bulging forearms, and short-cropped hair that couldn't hide a prematurely receding hairline, Montoya had been bestowed an inevitable nickname. The men of Destroyer 1 called their twenty-four-year-old lieutenant "Popeye." It can be tough for a young officer to gain the respect of the grizzled veterans under his command, but Montoya had already proved his courage under fire and, more importantly, was deemed to have good instincts.

"Popeye always showed a sharpness and a willingness to listen," says Sergeant Juan Carlos Rojas, his thirty-four-year-old second-in-command. "There's no point being tough if you don't have the talent to work things out and take the right decisions. We trusted him."

On the afternoon of May 17, Montoya had put that trust to the test. That afternoon, two men from Destroyer 1 were patrolling the quadrant when they spotted dark figures moving through the undergrowth. They squatted, raised their rifles, and pressed their eyes to the sights. "It was a critical moment," recalls Montoya. "My men were on combat footing, and they were ready to pull the trigger."

The soldiers remained motionless. Through the dense foliage, it was impossible to tell if the strangers were armed. When they were less than thirty meters away, they shouted out for the men to raise their hands above their heads and to come forward slowly. The startled faces of Manuel Ranoque, Henry Guerrero, and the rest of the Araracuara search team emerged from between the trees.

The men radioed news of the encounter back to Montoya at the base in the center of the search quadrant. The lieutenant knew he couldn't leave the men wandering around the search area. If they bumped into one of the other commando teams, things might not be settled so peacefully. He told them to bring the men in.

When they arrived, the first thing that struck Montoya was how poorly equipped the Indigenous were. They had machetes, but no hammocks to sleep in, and barely any food. Manuel had been wearing the same sweat-sodden black shirt for over a week. Henry Guerrero was walking around in a pair of battered sneakers. One of the soldiers fired up the gas stove and broke open a ration pack. Soon the men from Araracuara were sitting in a circle wolfing down pasta Alfredo from the steaming aluminum pouches.

Manuel asked to use the satellite phone; he needed it to call his psychic, he said. They watched as Manuel spoke a few words into the receiver, nodded several times in understanding, and then hung up. He turned to the soldiers and told them that 250 meters west of where they had found the baby's bottle they would find further evidence of the children.

Rojas, the dark and rangy machine-gunner, watched as his commanding officer took out his GPS, punched in some coordinates, and set off into the shadows with Manuel and a pair of Indigenous searchers. *How are we meant to explain to the operations base that we marched off on the orders of a psychic,* he thought to himself. *They'll think we're crazy—we're not meant to do this kind of thing.*

Two hours later, he saw Montoya return with a strange expression on his face. He went straight to the satellite phone and called San José del Guaviare. They had found children's footprints next to a stream, he said. "Great news, soldier, keep going, keep working hand in hand with the Indigenous," came the reply over the speaker. The mission, Rojas realized, was becoming unlike any he had been involved in.

As he spoke with the Indigenous that evening, Montoya's pity for their condition was soon replaced by admiration. They were a hardy, determined bunch, united by a shared cause, but there was something about Manuel—the intensity of his gaze, the pent-up energy of his body language—that was particularly striking. He told Montoya that he would not leave the jungle until he found his children. "He looked like a man with nothing to lose," recalls the soldier. It made him think of his own children in Bogotá. "I'm a father, too, and I knew that if I were in his position, I would make the same decision."

It was a moment of recognition and empathy between the hitherto competing search teams. Montoya wondered if they might be an asset to the search. He decided to sleep on it.

With the darkness closing in, he invited the Indigenous to stay in the camp that night. It was a serious breach of protocol. Commandos never allow strangers to sleep in their midst and Sergeant Rojas was wary.

That night, he told the men to be on high alert, to keep watch over the newcomers. "We kept our weapons in our sleeping bags, and made sure we left nothing lying around the camp," Rojas recalls. When his time for sentry duty came, he remembers keeping a close eye on Henry Guerrero when he rose from his tarp in the middle of the night, watching him through the trees as he made his way to the outskirts of the camp, where he relieved his bladder with a hearty sigh.

The next morning, Montoya invited the Indigenous to join the Destroyer 1 search team. During the day, the men from Araracuara marched with the soldiers as they completed their quadrant searches. In the evenings, Manuel Ranoque was invited to sit in on the daily radio reports as each military search group updated its progress. No one was more anxious to receive news and to understand how the wider search was progressing. The Indigenous were surprised at how welcoming the commandos were, how generous they were with the food and medicine, and how readily they shared information. "They were great guys," says Manuel. "They provided us with security, with food, and they helped us out. We walked together every day, and we became almost like friends."

Despite the ragged clothes and lack of supplies, the soldiers noted that there was an organization to the Indigenous search team that was similar to their own. They had an order of march, a navigator, and a medic. The difference was that the navigator worked with the sun rather than the GPS, and the medic employed the plants of the forest rather than pills and bandages.

The soldiers put these skills to the test. They asked the Indigenous to find, for example, a spot 300 meters to the northeast. They watched as the Uitoto and Muinane men took their bearings by the sun, identified a tree as a reference point, and began pacing out the distance. When the soldiers joined them at the spot and checked the GPS, they were rarely more than ten meters out.

Henry Guerrero showed particular enthusiasm for displaying the paisano know-how. He identified water-bearing creepers, and showed the soldiers how to extract the fluid; he also showed them to how to weave shelters from palm leaves that were almost impervious to the rain. On one occasion, he set off towards an unpromising-looking stream and returned with his arms full of sabaleta, which they cooked and shared between soldiers and the Indigenous units.

The biggest revelation, however, was mambé. The soldiers, who made a living out of taking down cocaine traffickers, were now invited to try coca leaves in their powdered form. The Indigenous men showed the soldiers how to moisten the mambé with saliva and poke it into the space between cheek and gum with their tongue. It was a sign of respect and acceptance. Across the Amazon and among the Uitoto communities in Colombia's big cities, a good bag of mambé is a source of pride and one of the best gifts one can give.

From then on, the soldiers patrolled with bulging cheeks. The wads of mambé acted as an appetite suppressant and a stimulant.

"It makes you feel really strong," says Montoya, pulling out a bag of the green powder from his bookshelf in Bogotá. "In the jungle, it really worked." The soldier they called Popeye was now fueled by the Uitotos' answer to spinach.

At night, while the soldiers rocked in their hammocks, the Indigenous would light a fire, distribute their mambé, and sit around talking in their native tongue. As it got later, Manuel's voice rose above all the others, sad and rhythmic, like a prayer. The next day, Montoya asked Henry Guerrero to tell them what they had talked about. Manuel had spoken of a fight with the spirits of the jungle that had devoured his children. Now he was asking for their return.

On May 23, ninety-two new Indigenous searchers entered the jungle. They included reinforcements from Araracuara, Nasa men from the Cauca region, and a group of ten Nukak, members of Colombia's last nomadic tribe. They were assigned to other commando teams, and their impact was immediate. By 5.00pm that afternoon, in an area just 500 meters from the crash site, the Nukak searchers located two diapers, a cell phone case, another palm shelter, and a pair of tiny blue sneakers.

The next day was Cristin's first birthday. Led by Manuel, the soldiers and Indigenous sang "Happy Birthday" to her in the camp.

Three days later, as the combined search team patrolled an area one kilometer west of where the baby's bottle had been found, one of the men from Araracuara called out. To the side, on the soft, muddy banks of a stream, were two footprints: one belonged to a child; the other, to an animal, possibly a dog. They seemed fresh, only a few days old, and not washed away by the rain. The soldiers had walked straight past them, but they had not escaped Uitoto eyes. Montoya had come to admire the tracking skills that his new companions possessed.

"We figured out that these guys were pretty strong," he says. "They taught us that there are a lot more techniques to jungle survival than we learned in the Special Forces."

The footprints added a new data point to the confused map of clues. The evidence of the children's survival had been found in two main clusters. The first was around the crash site itself, where the Nukak had found the diapers and the sneakers. The second was two kilometers west, where Dragon 4 had found the baby's bottle on May 15. The shelter, scissors, and the chewed juan soco fruit were all discovered close by. There were also isolated clues to the north and west of this cluster: another shelter, and one of the food kits dropped into the jungle that had been opened, but with its contents left untouched.

Another set of footprints had been located over two kilometers to the north. It seemed impossible that the children had been walking these distances while the search area was teeming with soldiers. The thick leaf cover on the floor and the effect of the rains made footprints difficult to detect, but it defied belief that the expert trackers in the search party hadn't found more evidence of the children's passage through the jungle.

Henry Guerrero had an explanation. On a couple of occasions, they had come across strange clearings in the otherwise thick vegetation. To Henry, these were the spiritual homes, the malocas, of the jungle spirits. He and other members of the Indigenous search team could sense their presence, the dark energy they emitted. He had reached an uncomfortable conclusion. The children had been taken by a *duende*.

Amazonian mythology is full of mystical beasts and malevolent spirits. Tree-dwelling forest guardians punish over-zealous hunters.

River-dwelling reptilian men cause sudden floods or lure young girls to a watery grave. Although the term duende comes from Spanish folklore, in the Amazon it refers to a shape-shifting spirit who befriends those lost in the jungle and offers them help, only to draw them deeper into the monte. Sometimes, it appears as an animal. Other times, it appears as a friend or loved one.

Henry shared his worrying theory with the soldiers. The children had escaped from the wreckage and made it as far as the spot where the baby's bottle had been found. It was there that they were captured by the duende, most probably taking the form of a tapir, which carried the children on its back. It whisked them from point to point, allowing them down to drink water from the stream. That explained why the children's footprints had been located at distant points. The duende fed and protected the children, but it was also poisoning their minds, making them discard the items they were carrying, and preventing them from calling out to the search parties.

A few kilometers away, the Dragon 4 team were patrolling when news of the duende theory made the rounds on army radio. Montiel turned to one of his commandos, a man who had grown up in the jungles of Caquetá, and asked him if he thought such a beast could really exist. "I know it does" was the unexpected reply.

With decreasing degrees of jest, the soldiers in Montiel's group came to attribute the strange goings-on in the forest to the acts of the duende. There was the time that their compasses started to spin aimlessly for an hour, causing them to lose their bearings and take an hour to cover one hundred meters. A soldier double-knotted his boots, only to find them untied again and again, as if plucked by a mischievous hand.

Other commando teams reported similar unexplained events.

Men would find themselves suddenly unable to take a step forward, as if they were being held back by an invisible force. Branches would inexplicably fall from the trees above them. At night, their hammocks would begin to swing for no reason, and the background noises of the jungle—birdsong and animal grunts—morphed into sinister human laughter. The soldiers began to succumb to malarial fevers and the tingling sensation of creeping leishmaniasis.

"I'm a Catholic, and we don't believe in these kinds of things," says Montiel cautiously. "But with what we went through there, if you ask me if evil exists, yes, it exists." Something, duende or not, seemed to want to impede the soldiers from completing their mission.

One afternoon, Montiel received orders to pick up a package from the helipad. Inside the cardboard box were four bottles of aguardiente Cristal, the local aniseed-flavored liquor. It was not an invitation to celebrate. The soldiers were to take the bottles to the point, just over a kilometer away, where two streams joined, forming a Y shape. At midnight, they were to put the bottles in the shape of a cross. The Indigenous belief, now supported by the military command, was that the duende would get drunk off the aguardiente and release the children.

That night, Destroyer 4 set off confidently; they had visited the Y-shaped stream before and had it logged on the GPS. "We had the point identified, but, would you believe it, that night we couldn't find it," explains Montiel, still nonplussed several months later. In the end, they arranged the bottles at the side of a stream, to no perceived effect on their fortunes.

In time, the one casualty of Operation Hope would become attributed to the actions of the duende. A week earlier, Wilson, one of the Belgian shepherd sniffer dogs, had broken free of his leash. It happened amid the thunderclaps and falling branches of a violent storm and, at first, his handler was not overly concerned. Wilson was among the military's best-trained dogs and an experienced jungle operator. He could sniff out landmines, abseil in a harness from helicopters, and stay calm and silent in combat situations. He had escaped his leash before, and would always return, panting and muddy-pawed.

This time, however, Wilson had not returned. In the following ten days, he was spotted twice by soldiers, first in the south-eastern-most corner of the search area, and then in its center, a kilometer north-west of the crash site. The second time he looked skinny, his ribs visible through his fur, and seemed highly agitated. When a soldier tried to approach him, he bolted in the opposite direction. As the men of Ares 3 cooked up sausages in the hope of attracting their companion back to camp, they wondered what could have caused Wilson's sudden change of character. The storm? A snake bite? An encounter with a jaguar? Or something else entirely?

As part of the new influx of volunteers announced by Yule, Montoya's team were set to be joined by five men from Puerto Leguízamo, a town on the Putomayo River. Among them was Eliécer Muñoz.

When I met him at a market in Suba, he was in Bogotá to complete his paperwork to register as a *desplazado*. He was forty-eight years old, with a thin moustache and round cheeks. He was short and strong, and as a youth he had served as a conscript in the Colombian army. The experience had not endeared him to the institutions of the state. Now he was a member of the local Indigenous Guard.

When he first heard about the disappearance of HK-2803, he told me, he had thought little of it. The passengers had been Indigenous, and, in his experience, the government paid little attention to the fate of its native peoples. In 2000, his father and only brother had been "disappeared" by armed groups. For three years, he had searched for them in the rivers and villages around Puerto Leguízamo, on the southern border with Peru. The state had offered him no support. He never found their bodies, so he was never able to give his loved ones a burial.

By mid-May, however, as Operation Hope ramped-up and confused journalists tried to explain the children's mysterious disappearance on the nightly news, Eliécer realized that the explanation lay outside the bounds of military expertise.

"When we saw on the news that there was no sign of the children, we began to worry," he remembers. "We knew already that the children had been taken by the Mother of the Jungle."

When he heard about the discovery of the baby's bottle, his mind was made up. The air force had sent a plane to take volunteers from Puerto Leguízamo to San José del Guaviare. There were four spaces reserved for members of the Indigenous Guard. Eliécer told his wife that he had to join the search. He had a gut feeling that only an Indigenous search team would be able to retrieve the children from the clutches of the jungle spirits.

On the night of May 28, General Pedro Sánchez was back in the CCOES's Bogotá office. Reports from the troops on the ground suggested that the integration of the Indigenous volunteers was progressing well. There were now close to 200 men traversing the search area, but the objects they had turned up had brought them no closer to finding the children. Above, the flyovers had yielded no new clues. There were no blips on the motion sensors. The Belgian shepherds had picked up no scents.

Never before had the Colombian state expended so much money, technology, and manpower on a civilian rescue mission. No one had said it to him directly, but Sánchez could tell that patience was running out among the military command. At one point, he had told one of their number the total cost for the operation to date (a figure that was never made public), and it made his colleague's eyes widen in disbelief. Sánchez refused to trim the spending, but he had the feeling that the money could be cut at any moment.

Meanwhile, public fascination with the case continued to grow. On the nightly news, Fatima said that she could sense the children were still alive, and let the Colombian nation in on the current dominant theory. "At this stage, it's not the children who are walking. Some of the animals from the monte must be carrying them—that's why they are no longer sitting still," she told RCN. "This animal that is transporting them, running in circles, is a duende, and this has me very worried."

Sánchez turned off the television and walked down the corridor to the regiment's tiny chapel, wedged in the corner of the building. It had floor-to-ceiling windows, four rows of narrow pews, and a small lectern. Over the course of the search, he had found himself visiting this peaceful spot with increasing frequency. With his men looking to him for direction, and the media gaze frequently upon him, it was his chosen spot for solitary contemplation and, on occasion, where he would let out tears of frustration and despair.

That week, his ten-year-old son had been given a school assignment. He had to draw his hero, and he had drawn his dad, the man who would find the children in the jungle. "I told myself that I couldn't fail the children, or the child who had made that drawing," he remembers.

As he sat in the pew, however, his prayers were infected by a sense of desperation. "One imagines that sometimes God gives you a sign," he says. "But that day, I read the Bible, I looked under the pews, I looked at the ceiling and out the window towards the streets. I asked Him, what have I done wrong? In what way have we failed?"

Then, his hands clenched together, he asked the children to forgive him.

On the flight to San José del Guaviare, Eliécer was worried. As the senior member of the four-man team from Puerto Leguízamo, it would fall to him to perform the rituals to convene with the spirits and to open the jungle for the search team. The previous evening, he had received instructions from one of the village elders about which prayers to recite, which words to speak to the unfamiliar jungle of the Apaporis. As he stared out over the forest below, he felt the weight of this responsibility. He wished there was someone to share the burden with.

When the plane touched down and the passengers disembarked, Eliécer saw a familiar figure waiting by the helicopter. He felt a sense of relief, as if his prayers had been answered. Here was a man whose spiritual connection with the jungle was the stuff of local legend.

"Don Rubio!" he called out.

CHAPTER SEVENTEEN

The Vine of the Soul

When José Rubio Rodríguez was nine years old, his grandfather took him to an underground cavern deep in the jungle. A colony of bats hung from the ceiling. The high-pitch clicking of *guácharos,* a cave-dwelling Amazonian bird, echoed from the damp stone walls. His grandfather sat him down and laid out the plants and vines he had brought with him on the ground. Young Rubio's apprenticeship had begun.

When we first meet in September 2023 Rubio is fifty-five, with an athletic gait and long limbs. He has narrow, penetrating eyes, and the tops of his ears point out from his head. His large hands move swiftly and fluidly to illustrate his points. His voice is still hoarse from the jungle, giving him additional gravitas. The Uitoto speak about his unmatched knowledge of the jungle with reverence. They call him Don Rubio, a form of address reserved for those of high social standing. He had joined the search at the request of Manuel Ranoque and Magdalena's parents. There was no one better equipped to deal with the duende. Don Rubio was a man who had dedicated his life to convening with the dark spirits of the jungle. And it had all begun in that cave, at the feet of his grandfather.

Bartolo Rodríguez was a solitary, melancholy man. As a child, he and his Uitoto clan had been enslaved by the rubber barons. He had seen family members tortured for failing to collect their quota of latex, women raped and men garroted. Bartolo had rebelled, killing several of his captors and escaping into the jungle under fire from the guards. One of the bullets found its mark, penetrating his abdomen, but Bartolo, in Rubio's telling, had a "body like the figure eight." The projectile passed straight through him, missing all his internal organs, leaving only dark scars and a lifelong fear of firearms. He'd escaped to the banks of the Caquetá River to plot revenge on the Peruvian rubber workers. But vengeance never came. He grew old, and his two sons became men and left the jungle. He'd seen his people massacred and his culture brought to the precipice of extinction. Only his grandson remained.

"He told me he had no kind of life until I was born," remembers Rubio of their conversations in the cave. "He chose me, and he told me everything." Bartolo and his wife had cared for him since he was six months old. They raised him on the fruits, nuts, and juices of the monte. Rubio began to take mambé when he was just seven, around the time that he learned his clan's songs in their native language. The real work, however, began in damp and the dark, with the bats and the *guácharos*. "Whether you want to be a curer, a shaman, or a narrator of traditional stories, before you can practice in the maloca, you have to study in the jungle, in the caves, under the trees," he explains.

They spent two weeks talking, eating, and sleeping in the cave. Rubio absorbed his people's ancestral knowledge through the siphon of his grandfather. When they finally left, he had learned many of the plant remedies for the jungle's ailments, and by the age of ten he was considered a *curandero*, a medicine man. At fifteen, he performed his first ritual, communing with the jungle spirits: the tiger, the boa, the bear, and the eagle.

When the helicopter carrying him and the men from Puerto Leguízamo touched down at the jungle helipad, Don Rubio asked to be taken first to the site of the wreckage. The men from the Puerto Leguízamo search team stood by, their cheeks filled with mambé as he began his ritual. "I focused on the spirits of the jungle, the animals," he recalls. "I asked permission to enter. I told them we weren't there to destroy nature or to kill animals, just to take back our family. Above all, I asked for good weather, that it be like summer."

He called on the jungle spirits to spare the area to the north, east, and west from heavy rains, and to push the heavy clouds to the south. For the next week, the rains relented. Unlike the men from Araracuara, Eliciér, Don Rubio, and the other men from Puerto Leguízamo kept their distance from the soldiers in Montoya's Destroyer 1 team. "You have to understand that we have been badly beaten by the system," Eliécer explains. "We didn't want the soldiers watching over us, especially our rituals. We stayed over here, and they stayed over there."

It took a bout of flu to warm relations. When several men from the Puerto Leguízamo team came down with severe headaches, Sergeant Rojas gave them antibiotics, and cooked them up a steaming cup of panela, the local sugarcane drink. "That established trust," says Eliécer. "Little by little, we got closer, living together, sharing food." Only Don Rubio, silent and solitary on the fringes of the group, kept his distance from the soldiers. He had inherited his grandfather's suspicion of guns. As he walked, he was overawed by what he sensed around him. "In the Caquetá, the spirits are light," he says. "There, in the Apaporis, in the virgin forest, they were heavy, they were malign."

On June 3, it was time for the first three CCOES teams to

leave the jungle. At the helipad, a Black Hawk was waiting to ferry them for a week of rest and recovery. The men of Destroyer 1 were looking forward to hot showers, air conditioning, and grilled meat.

The search area was now a vastly different place from the pristine jungle they had dropped into four weeks earlier. There were sixteen Special Forces teams and seventy-three indigenous volunteers on the ground. At the spot where the baby bottle had been found, a giant floodlight had been set up. Six loudspeakers now replayed Fatima's message around the clock. Eleven kilometers of florescent-yellow construction tape had been stretched through the trees to catch the attention of the children as they moved. Along their length hung 2,200 plastic whistles.

At the helipad, the men posed for a final photo, commandos and Indigenous standing side-by-side. In the middle, a shirtless Manuel Ranoque, his hair now long and thick, held one corner of the Colombian flag; Lieutenant Montoya held the other. Henry Guerrero presented Sergeant Rojas with a gift he'd made: a pair of palm leaves tightly woven together that symbolized the unification of the two search teams. As Rojas shouldered his rucksack, Manuel approached him, almost tearful, and embraced him for what seemed an age. "Don't forget about us," the Uitoto man implored. Rojas assured him that they would return in a week.

As the pilot began his pre-flight checks, Don Rubio abandoned his aloofness and approached Montoya. He had a final request. Montoya took out his notebook and wrote down names. Then he boarded the Black Hawk, and the men from Puerto Leguízamo and Araracuara stepped back towards the trees to watch it rise, tilt its nose forward and disappear from sight.

In the back of the helicopter, Sergeant Rojas felt a knot

of disappointment in his stomach, the feeling of a mission unaccomplished. "It was disheartening," he recalls. "We'd been searching every day from morning to night, and we still didn't have the answer, we barely had a clue."

At San José del Guaviare, Montoya rushed straight to the operations base and tracked down Captain Armando Guerrero, the head of logistics. It was imperative, he said, that they deliver several doses of yagé, a powerful psychedelic vine, to Don Rubio.

"This could be the key to completing the mission, to finding the children," he told him.

As the head of logistics, Captain Guerrero had his work cut out. In addition to supplying sixteen commando teams, he had also been tasked with sourcing items for the Indigenous that were not to be found in army warehouses. In the last week, he had used Giovani Yule's contacts to source ambil and mambé supplies, and he'd sent a soldier to the local store for the bottles of aguardiente required for the duende ritual. Now, no request seemed too outlandish.

"Any idea, no matter how crazy it seemed, was now on the table," he recalls. "It may have seemed wacky to us, but now all we had was hope and faith that it would work."

In one corner of Araracuara, at the end of a jungle path, a cluster of houses surrounded a small dirt soccer field. A little further on, nestled in a grove of fruit trees and overlooking a small stream, was Serafina Guerrero's house.

Serafina was Henry Guerrero's aunt. She was in her seventies, with a wide nose and long earlobes, and she kept her dark hair pinned up with a plastic clip. She was a matriarch of the Guerrero clan. From her house, she could hear the shouts and squeals of a dozen Uitoto girls kicking a deflated ball around on the soccer field. They were all her granddaughters and great-granddaughters.

Serafina's long kitchen stood at the back of the house. Dozens of metal pots were stacked on shelves or hung from hooks. In the corner, suspended over a wood stove, was a wire mesh containing the smoked heads of fish and chunks of meat. The kitchen smelled of smoke, and the wooden walls were stained black by it.

From the kitchen, it was only a short walk down a set of steep wooden stairs to the garden. There were trees bearing green plantains, milpeso palms, and pineapple bushes. In a small plot nearest the house was a thick bush. The leaves were dark green and tear-shaped, and from them grew a thick, pale liana, knotted like a girl's plaited ponytail. It was *banisteriopsis caapi*, or yagé, as the People of the Center called it. In the Amazon of Peru and among its many Western devotees, it is better known as ayahuasca, a hispanicized Quechua word meaning "vine of the soul."

At sunrise on June 5, Serafina cut eight knots from one of the lianas. In the kitchen, she followed the preparation technique her mother had taught her when she was a child. She boiled and pulverized the cutting before hanging it from a nail on the wall, positioning a collection bowl underneath to capture the drips. When the liana gave no more water, she heated it again in the collected liquid and hung it once more, repeating the process until the liquid was thick and viscous.

Then she decanted the mixture into a 600-milliliter soda bottle and screwed on the cap. There was enough for two doses. The potent brew was ferried from Araracuara to San José del Guaviare by Natalya Rodríquez, a cousin of Herman Mendoza, who delivered it to Captain Guerrero. She told him that this was the last hope for the search mission.

Guerrero picked up the plastic bottle and turned it slowly,

observing how the thick, dark liquid stuck to the sides. "So this is yagé?" he said.

Yagé is native to the Napo Valley of Ecuador, where it is known as "the mother of all plants." For centuries, the curanderos of the valley have used the vine to help them understand the medicinal properties of forest plants. Yagé's main active ingredients are monoamine oxidase inhibitors (MAOIs). The effect of these molecules is to make the curandero more sensitive to the effects of jungle plants when they are mixed and cooked with yagé. It helps him to understand their purpose and to imagine how they could be used to treat disease.

When Spanish conquistadors introduced malaria to the Amazon, it took just twenty-five years for Ecuadoran curanderos to discover that the bark of the quinine-rich cinchona tree could be consumed to fight the disease.

Yagé was spread throughout the Amazon by humans, planted on fallow chagras to ensure it received ample sunlight. In many Indigenous societies, it is used to treat diseases. A curandero might take it to diagnose a patient's illness, or prescribe a powerful dose to a patient in order to bring on a purge. Yagé's active ingredients cause vomiting and defecation, but many claim that the process has helped them overcome physical and emotional traumas, and leaves them feeling cleansed from the inside out. Some shamans refer to this form as boa yagé, after the snake.

When combined with other plants, however, yagé can bring on powerful psychedelic episodes. Leaves from the chakruna and the chaliponga plants contain dimethyltryptamine (DMT), a powerful hallucinogenic that is usually broken down by the stomach lining. The vine's active ingredients inhibit this process and allow the DMT to become active.

This is tiger yagé, and it is used by shamans for divination and remote viewing. While these days the Indigenous can make videocalls wherever an adequate internet service exists, in the past they might have entrusted a shaman to take tiger yagé to gain an insight into the life of a friend or relative long departed from the jungle. Warriors would take yagé to identify where their enemies were hiding in the jungle, and hunters would use it to locate prey. Given the right dose, they believe, the soul leaves the limitations of the body, moves through the forest, and becomes one with the jaguar. The Tukanos and other tribes native to the Apaporis basin consume tiger yagé regularly in ceremonies to Yuruparí, their mythical hero.

Yagé is not as central to Uitoto culture. It appears in the cosmology, where the vine is represented as an umbilical cord to the universe, linking man to the ground below and the heavens above, but most People of the Center go through their lives without tasting it.

In nearly forty years as a curandero, Don Rubio had prescribed dozens of plant-based treatments to the sick and wounded paisanos of the Caquetá-Putumayo basin. But he had administered yagé on only a handful of occasions, usually when his patient was in their final, agonizing hours. "That's when you use yagé, as the final resort," he says. "It's God, it's the creator."

The soda bottle made its way to the jungle in the company of military top brass. On June 7, after a month coordinating the search from San José del Guaviare and Bogotá, General Pedro Sánchez touched down in the jungle of the Apaporis for the first time. He wanted to check that his orders were being carried out correctly on the ground, to take the measure of the troops' morale, and to reconfirm the CCOES's commitment to the cause. "I was determined to complete the mission," he told me later. "But, at that point, I thought we would find them dead."

When he asked the commandos how they were doing, professional pride dictated their response. They were fine, they said, but Sánchez could tell they were tired. The energy of the first weeks had gone. He sent orders to bring in new commandos from Cali. Meanwhile, the Indigenous volunteers were beginning to depart. Over a dozen boarded the helicopter that Sánchez had arrived in. From a peak of ninety-two volunteers, only sixteen remained in the jungle. The Indigenous had earmarked June 10 as the final day of their search efforts—if the children were not found by then, they reasoned, it meant that the duende's grip was too strong. They would be lost to the jungle forever.

On the ground, Sánchez saw with his own eyes the difficulties of the terrain. It was impossible to see more than ten meters ahead. If they had to do a total rake of the search area, he realized, it would take many months. At night, while he lay in his hammock, it was so dark that he couldn't see his hand six inches from his face. "I felt overwhelmed by the immensity of it all," he says. "I had a sense of subordination to something much bigger."

A few hundred meters away, Don Rubio had come into possession of the bottle of yagé. He had built a small lean-to shelter from palms in a clearing close to the wreckage of the Cessna. It would provide the silence and seclusion necessary for visions to take root. Manuel watched anxiously as Rubio poured half the mixture into a plastic cup.

For the best effect, it was vital that the yagé be taken by someone with a strong personal connection to the children. Manuel, Rubio had decided, was the only one in a position to request their return from the forest spirits. He passed him the cup, and watched as he swallowed the bitter potion and lay down in the shelter.

Manuel had taken yagé before. He says that when Tien was nine months old, Magdalena had fallen sick, and he had traveled to Chukiki to seek advice from Fatima. She had instructed him to take yagé, to push through the purge and focus his mind on one single thing: the health of his girlfriend. He knew that yagé was both good and evil. It could help bring you closer to the forest spirits, but it could also show you the unvarnished truth about yourself, "as if on a television screen."

As he lay in the shelter and the yagé passed into his body, Manuel couldn't concentrate. He says he was tortured by thoughts of Magdalena's death, by the threats he had faced from the guerrillas, and by the strange, wild monte he was lying in. As he lay there, sweating, his head spinning, he reached the conclusion that he wasn't the right person to perform the ritual. It needed someone more experienced, he says, someone with the knowledge of a curandero and who knew how to talk to the spirits.

Ten minutes after taking the yagé, Manuel was back on his feet. The mixture was bad, he complained. He hadn't seen anything, and, besides, it would be better for Rubio to make the connection with the duende. But Rubio was angry. Manuel hadn't opened himself to the process. Eliécer watched as the two men argued.

"You have to be prepared, mentally and spiritually, and you have to know the reason you are taking it," he recalls. "Manuel doubted himself—that's why he didn't see. He lacked the truth."

The next morning, as the Indigenous from Puerto Leguízamo sat around the camp, Eliécer turned to Rubio.

"It's down to you," he said.

"I'll take it tonight," Rubio replied. "I'll tell you if I see the duende or not. If I don't, it's time to leave." He told Eliécer to prepare the men from Puerto Leguízamo for a final day's searching. Then he spent the rest of the day preparing his mind.

At midnight, as he began to prepare the next batch of yagé, Rubio already knew he would find the children. He could hear them talking, he says, and hear them crying. At three o'clock on the morning of June 9, he lay down in the shelter and drank the last of the bottle.

"When you take yagé, you go to the creator—we call him Mo Buinaima," he says. "You go above and you look down below. I told him that I couldn't take it anymore, that the duende was beating me. I asked him to show me where the children were, and he did. Then he sent me back to Earth, to where I had to wrestle with evil. I walked in darkness, I felt like I was dead. It was just my soul that was walking."

As his spirit traveled the jungle, he felt the presence of the duende. He felt its touch on his skin. He turned and saw him. He took the form of a human: dark-skinned and naked, with a pot belly and a hairy chest.

"We stood face to face," recounts Rubio, "as clear as if we were meeting in the street." The duende asked him what he was doing, and he told him he was looking for the children. *They're mine*, the duende told him. It had no intention of releasing them; it wanted to convert them into fellow duendes. If Rubio wanted to take them, he would have to deal with the consequences.

"He grabbed me by the throat, as if to strangle me, then he threw me against a tree trunk. Then I woke up."

It was 5.00am. He knew where the children were.

When dawn broke, Eliécer assembled a team of Indigenous Guard from the now-dwindling ranks of the searchers. Rubio told them that the children were 2.5 kilometers away and that they would find them before the day was out. The soldiers readied themselves to leave, but Rubio told them he would only walk in a purely Indigenous group.

At midday, they stopped to drink and take mambé. Eliécer had been suffering from fevers and had been subsisting on a diet of hot chocolate. Some of the group turned back, leaving Eliécer and his three companions from Puerto Leguízamo: Nicolás Ordóñez, Dairo Kumariteke and Edwin Manchola. There were still four hours of light left in the day—the last four hours in which to find the missing children.

Two hours later, they met with a propitious sign. Lumbering across their path was a red-footed tortoise, the local equivalent of a genie in a bottle. According to local lore, ask it a wish and you shall receive, as long as the turtle is subsequently set free. Eliécer picked it up by the shell. "You're going to deliver me to the children," he said. "And if you don't, I'll eat your liver." Raising the stakes further for the unfortunate reptile, Nicolas Ordoñez promised to drink its blood. Eliécer made a pouch by weaving together the fronds of a palm. He inserted the turtle and carried it over his shoulder.

An hour later, their wish was granted. They heard the sound of a baby crying.

CHAPTER EIGHTEEN

Miracle

Lesly lay on the ground under the mosquito net and sucked on milpeso seeds, but even that effort seemed to absorb more energy than she had left. She rubbed her foot against her ankle, seeking relief from the irritating insect bites.

For nine days, the children had remained in the small clearing, following the flier's instructions. She had watched her siblings grow thinner and gaunter by the day. Tien could no longer stand up, but Soleiny still had the strength to hold Cristin. As she did so, she picked at her left wrist where the leishmaniasis had spread, forming yellowish ulcers. Lesly reached out and gently pressed her sister's hand to stop her scratching. Then her own arm fell limply back by her side.

A few days earlier, as they were sitting in the clearing, a dog had come through the undergrowth. It had a black snout and brown fur, under which its ribs protruded like the keys of a xylophone. It approached the children inquisitively, and sat with them. They watched it, unsure if the dog was real. Later, as darkness was setting in, the children heard a low growling that seemed to surround them. Lesly recognized the sound. It was a pack of *perros del monte*, the wild short-eared dogs that prowl the Amazon. The Belgian shepherd's ears pricked up, and he disappeared, snarling, into the undergrowth.

Afterwards, as she looked around the area for fruit trees, she had felt panic rise up through her body like a wave of cold water. Her chest had tightened, her breath suddenly short and sharp. Her heart had pounded in her chest, and she had found herself drenched in sweat. She had lain down in the shelter, and she hadn't moved since. Lesly's thoughts were calm now.

She thought of the chagra, with its manioc and plantains. She thought of the animals of the monte—the tapirs and snakes, the huge red tortoise that had passed by the clearing a few days ago. She thought of her mother.

She heard a sound in the undergrowth, and she tried to imagine which jungle predator might be stalking them. Cristin let out a wail. Lesly gathered her last strength and got to her feet, pulling at Soleiny's arm and ushering her towards the undergrowth. She heard a man call out and the sound of branches snapping, and of feet pounding on the ground. Around the children, dark forms seemed to flicker behind the dense vegetation. Then they heard voices in her Uitoto tongue.

"Lesly, we're family," they said.

The men came closer, spreading their arms like goalkeepers, encircling them and moving slowly inwards. They were wearing blue T-shirts with black vests. They crouched before the children, smiled, and spoke to them softly.

Tien, still sitting in the clearing, looked up at one of the men and said: "My mom died."

The men gathered them around the shelter. One of them had a red tortoise strapped to his back in a palm basket. As they looked at the children, their faces grew drawn with concern. They lit tobacco and blew soft billows of smoke over the children. One of them took Cristin in his arms and sang a gentle lullaby.

Lesly grew in confidence.

"I'm hungry," she told the men. But the oldest man, the one they called Eliécer, told her that it was too dangerous for her to eat right now. They gave her a sip of agua panela that they carried in a flask.

Each man picked up a child in his arms. Lesly went with the one they called Nicolás, who was young and strong and wore a green bandana on his head. They began to walk and run through the jungle. After an hour, they were exhausted. Soleiny wouldn't stop asking for food. Finally, Eliécer sat her down and opened his pack. He removed some fariña and some fried sausages, and passed them to the children. It tasted delicious. Eliécer crossed himself and looked up towards the narrow glints of light that shone through the canopy.

"Forgive me, Lord," he said, "but if you didn't take their lives in the accident, why would you take them now with this little bit of food."

Nicolás and Eliécer stayed there with Lesly and Soleiny while the other two men dashed off into the jungle carrying Tien and Cristin. Twenty minutes later, two men in olive uniforms arrived, their rifles slung over their shoulders, their expressions a strange mix of delight and concern. They hoisted Lesly and Soleiny onto their shoulders and set off back in the direction they had come from.

When they set her down on the green plastic sheet, Lesly saw more men in uniform. One held Cristin, while another was spooning Tien soup from a black mug. One of the soldiers ran his hands over Lesly's arms and legs, checking for fractures. She winced when he got to her left calf.

A man with three yellow stripes on his arm set the radio on the ground and spoke into the transmitter in a trembling, excited voice.

"Miracle! Miracle! Miracle! Miracle!"

The rest of the men began to hack away at the trees with machetes. The children drank soup and sipped from the pouches of hydrating fluids that the soldiers had given them. A group of Indigenous arrived. Lesly saw her stepfather, Manuel, crying and shaking. He took Cristin in his arms and pressed her to his chest. He sat down on one of the tarps laid out on the ground and pulled Tien onto his lap. To his side, Lesly and Soleiny huddled under a blue blanket.

It was dark by the time the helicopter arrived, and rain was falling heavily. The soldiers removed clear plastic tubes from their pockets. They bent them in half and shook them, and they began to glow brightly, casting strange shadows throughout the jungle. Others pointed the beams of their torches upwards. The soldiers had cleared a space in the canopy with their machetes, and for the first time in weeks, Lesly could see the sky. The heavy clouds were illuminated by the moon and the lights from the helicopter, which hovered above, buffeted by the winds.

She watched as two men descended slowly towards the forest floor, sitting on a T-bar that was attached to a metal cable. Manuel went first, carrying Cristin tightly in his arms. One of the men strapped him in, and then took the other spot on the T-bar before both men were winched up into the sky and out of sight. The man from the helicopter returned to the ground. Tien went next, and then Soleiny.

Finally, it was Lesly's turn. The man put her legs in the harness and pulled the straps around her thighs. He told her to hold on to him tightly. As she rose through the forest, she felt the cold wind against her, and the rain lashing at her face. Then a strong hand grabbed her and pulled her into the body of the aircraft. She felt the helicopter rise and spin in the night sky. She looked around.

There were more men in uniform, as well as nurses in orange jackets. And there, at the back of the helicopter, Manuel was staring back at her.

PART III

THE CHILDREN
OF THE JUNGLE

CHAPTER NINETEEN

Two Colombias

In 2021, a huge billboard was unveiled over the Gran Via, Madrid's most important commercial street. Towering over the shoppers and tourists in the Spanish capital was the image of a girl with dark, curly hair, a turquoise skirt, and a luminous yellow butterfly in the palm of her hand. "Oh, Colorful Christmas," read the accompanying slogan.

Mirabel Madrigal was the star of Disney's latest animated movie, *Encanto*, which told the story of a Colombian family blessed with extraordinary abilities. One of the children could will plants to grow, another could control the weather with her emotions, and a third could speak to wild animals. One mischievous character even possessed a duende-like ability to shape-shift into other people.

Colombians loved *Encanto*. It showcased the gorgeous landscapes of the country's coffee zone, made a big deal of the local cuisine, and featured a soundtrack of Colombian artists that would top the Billboard 200 chart for nine weeks. Above all, it painted the country as a mysterious, magical place where a humble, loving people struggled against the odds.

Even as the children were on board the helicopter, flying out of the jungle, the Colombian press were piecing together a story that seemed straight out of the world of *Encanto*. The first photos of the children, wrapped in tarps, receiving food from their rescuers, were published online. They had endured forty days alone in one of the world's most hostile environments. It was an incredible feat of survival, a testament to sibling love and to the resourcefulness and fortitude of their Uitoto culture. Shortly before 7.00pm, Gustavo Petro posted on X: "A joy for all the country! The four children who were lost in the jungle have been found alive!" The rescue was confirmed. Colombia would be front-page news around the world, this time for the right reasons.

Because the "Colorful Christmas" promised on the *Encanto* billboard had been a dig at another show set in Colombia. Five years previously, at a site a few blocks away, Netflix had erected an advertisement for its show *Narcos*, about the Drug Enforcement Administration's efforts to break up the Medellín Cartel. Next to a shadowy picture of the actor who portrayed Pablo Escobar was the tagline "Oh, White Christmas." It was the sort of blasé and unfunny reference to cocaine that makes Colombians roll their eyes. *Narcos*, however, became a worldwide hit, and prompted a new generation of international viewers to associate the country with cartels and guerrillas. Colombians wondered if they would ever escape the shadow of their recent past.

The truth, of course, is that *Encanto* and *Narcos* portray two realities of a complex, beautiful, and sometimes violent country. As more details of the children's story began to emerge, these two Colombias collided.

Major Julian Novoa steered the Black Hawk north, under a moonless sky. He was returning from the most unexpected and high-profile mission of his career. That afternoon, he had been attending his unit's anniversary celebrations in Villavicencio. For weeks, he'd ferried soldiers and Indigenous back and forth from the jungle, but by June 9 expectations of finding the children alive had sunk so low that both of the Black Hawks had been withdrawn to the city at the foot of the Andes for routine maintenance. As he stood in file, watching medals being handed out, his commanding officer called him on his cell phone. "We have an evacuation," he said. The chain of command requires pilots to learn the details of their mission only shortly before takeoff. But there was no mistaking the emotion in the commander's voice. It was the children.

Novoa rushed to the runway on an electric scooter, where he waved the maintenance teams away from the Black Hawk and boarded his crew. The flight to Calamar usually took seventy minutes, but he pushed the nose forward steeply and made it in fifty-five. For a half an hour, as the rain buffeted the side of the aircraft, he held the helicopter steady over the tiny clearing that the ground troops had cut. Now he was returning home with a precious cargo. The blinking lights of the runway at San José del Guaviare appeared on the dark horizon.

On the ground, General Pedro Sánchez looked towards the sky. At his side were two Indigenous elders, one wearing the round hat of the Nasa people and the other the brightly feathered headdress of the Siona. Four hours earlier, the word "miracle" had echoed around the base. It was heard first through the radio static in the communications room, where the bleary-eyed radio operators looked at each other in disbelief. It was repeated in the operations room, where the intelligence analysts pounded their desks with their fists and veteran soldiers wept tears of relief. A few minutes later, in the upstairs conference room, Sánchez was in a meeting when one of his senior officers burst through the doors.

"Miracle," he said.

"Are they alive?" was the general's first response, not trusting the man's broad grin. At this stage, Sánchez had reached the painful conclusion that the search would most likely end with the discovery of the children's remains. "I couldn't believe it when he told me they were alive," he recalls. "I hugged him and told him, 'Thank you, thank you.'"

Now, in the warm and humid night, he watched in amazement as the children, wrapped in yellow space blankets, were taken from the helicopter and rushed to a military airplane that stood waiting on the runway. He followed them into the hold of the plane. Inside, the medics checked the children's vital signs and helped them slowly sip from bottles of isotonic drinks. He couldn't believe how frail they were. Cristin's arms, once so chubby, were painfully thin as she reached from her blanket to grasp for food.

"Well done, commandos, you made the impossible possible," he told his men. The two Indigenous elders entered the hold. They blew tobacco smoke over the children and prayed, a final ceremony to cleanse them of the jungle spirits that still clung to them. When they were done, Sánchez and the elders disembarked, and the plane prepared for takeoff. The general stood on the runway, watching in silence until it disappeared into the night sky.

On June 10, a taxi carrying Andrés Jacobombaire, his brother Jairo and his sister Rosamira pulled up in front of Bogotá's military hospital. In the shadow of the towering brutalist building, the reporters and camera crews formed a jostling crowd, hungry for any news about the children. The family passed through the metal detectors and made their way along the corridor to the pediatric ward, where a soldier stood guard outside the children's room. A nurse approached and told Andrés and his siblings that Lesly was waiting for their visit. Andrés felt weak. He leaned heavily on Jairo for support as the nurse pushed the door open. There in the bed lay Lesly, the daughter he hadn't seen for over six years. She sat up in bed and exclaimed: "*Papa!*"

As he slowly went to her bedside, Andrés began to cry. They were tears of relief and happiness, he told me afterwards, but also of pity for the state he found her in. Lesly's face was drawn, the gash on the right side of her head was open and pink, and the bones were visible in her forearms. When he lifted the blanket, he felt a rush of fear. She looked like a corpse, he remembers. Andrés hugged his daughter and told her he was proud of her, that she was a *guerrera*, a warrior. "It was hard, Papa, really hard," Lesly replied.

Soleiny, in the next bed, woke from her sleep. The children were too weak to speak about their ordeal in that first meeting with their father. They would remain in the hospital for over a month as they slowly regained weight on their preferred diet of soup and fariña, while the medical staff treated their injuries. In addition to the cut to her head, Lesly was suffering from a fungal infection, and both she and her sister had contracted leishmaniasis on their arms.

The skin-eating disease had taken its toll on the search parties, too. Along the corridor from the pediatric ward, nurses were attending to the oozing sores of dozens of soldiers and Indigenous volunteers. Some of the Uitoto had initially returned to Araracuara, but the local clinic lacked the microscopes needed to diagnose the disease, and they had been transferred to Bogotá. Members of the search parties had sustained other injuries and ailments—deep cuts, respiratory infections, the occasional broken bone—but the most unfortunate injury had befallen Nestor

Andoke, the hunter who had been among the party that found the plane. He'd slipped in the jungle and landed on a particularly sharp branch that had pierced his scrotum. It was an injury that he had tried to walk off, and one that horrified the commando medic when Andoke eventually offered himself for examination.

In the waiting rooms and in the hospital carpark, such anecdotes from the search parties—often heroic, occasionally gory—provided a dash of color for the reporters, but they didn't answer the burning question: *How had the children survived?*

Narciso Mucutuy offered the first account. Emerging from the ward with Fatima, he recounted what the children had told him. They'd survived on fariña at first, he said, and then on the fruits and seeds of the jungle. After losing the bottle, they had only fed Cristin water. The children had been cold and hungry, but they hadn't been scared, he said. They'd been comfortable in the jungle, and Lesly had relied on the skills she had learned from her parents and grandmother. For the moment, this answer, the only one available, would have to do. A most illustrious visitor had arrived.

On the day the children were rescued, President Gustavo Petro was returning from Havana, where he had been negotiating a potential peace deal with the ELN, another of Colombia's guerrilla groups. He visited the hospital the next day, accompanied by his wife and fifteen-year-old daughter. Afterwards, he posted photos on X showing him at the children's bedside, and praised the combined knowledge and efforts of the Indigenous and military search teams. He couldn't resist making a political point. The image of the Black Hawk helicopter, the quintessential symbol of Colombia's protracted internal conflict, being deployed to rescue the country's most vulnerable citizens was too powerful to ignore. "Here is a new Colombia," he wrote, "in which life comes before everything. The goal that unites us is life." Lesly and her siblings, he told reporters, would be remembered as "the children of peace."

Even the president's most unrelenting critics found it difficult to quibble with that sentiment. In the coming days and weeks, the Indigenous and military search teams and the children's relatives were special guests on TV shows and podcasts, and were liberally quoted in newspaper articles. In the tireless and brave men of Araracuara and Puerto Leguízamo, Colombia had new heroes. And in the humble words and youthful face of General Pedro Sánchez, the army had a new image. The story, with its unexpected happy ending, had delighted the public. It was all anyone seemed to talk about. In Bogotá cafes, gaggles of upper-class women could be overheard discussing the spiritual benefits of yagé. At building sites, shirtless construction workers lamented the fate of the search dog Wilson.

When the army announced that the search for the missing canine would continue, none of the country's opinion-makers were brave enough to question whether this was the best allocation of state resources. Under pressure from an expectant population, Operation Hope entered a third phase: the search for Wilson. "Our commitment as commandos is to never leave a fallen companion on the battlefield," General Helder Giraldo Bonilla, the chief of the armed forces, announced on X. In the coming two weeks, fifty ground troops and twenty logistical staff remained in the jungle, looking for the Belgian shepherd. All sorts of delicious, odorous recipes were cooked to try to attract him. Appealing to other canine instincts, several bitches in heat were dropped into the jungle.

In hospital, the children were given crayons and paper. Lesly drew mountains, a river, and trees, at the base of which was a brown dog. Soleiny's also featured a dog, along with flowers and a Colombian flag on a mast.

As requests to interview the children streamed in, the Colombian Institute of Family Welfare (ICBF) made the decision to forbid media access to them, arguing that they were in a frail state, both physically and emotionally. Until they had recovered, the Colombian public would not receive answers to their many questions, the most pressing of which were *How had the children been able to survive for forty days?* and *Why had the Colombian Special Forces been unable to locate them?* In the media blackout, legitimate curiosity became tangled up in politicized conspiracy theories.

Not everyone believes in miracles.

At 6.48pm on June 9, Lieutenant Colonel Óscar Dávila, a member of the presidential security team, made a call from the back seat of a Nissan SUV in central Bogotá. He was overjoyed, the family member who took the call said later, at the news of the children's rescue from the jungle. Dávila was one of millions of Colombians enjoying the cathartic moment, honking their car horns and calling their loved ones. But five minutes later he was dead, killed by a bullet to the temple.

A week earlier, Dávila had agreed to testify as a key witness in a major government corruption case. The case itself was as convoluted as a typical Colombian soap opera, featuring a thieving nanny, illegal phone-taps, and alleged shady donations to President Petro's election campaign. When Petro took to social media the next day to call Dávila's death a suicide, in advance of the coroner's report, his many fervent opponents smelled a *cortina de humo*, a smokescreen.

There were many curious details about Dávila's death that aroused suspicion. For many Colombians, his behavior and actions on June 9 didn't seem consistent with someone on the verge of suicide. Aside from his apparent buoyant mood only minutes before his death, that morning he'd paid a lawyer $12,000 to represent him. The gun that killed Dávila had been left in the car by his driver-bodyguard when he had gone to buy a bottle of water; this was implausible to some private security experts, who pointed out that the first rule of the job is to never be separated from one's firearm. To many, however, it was the timing of his death that was too convenient to be a coincidence. The government, they alleged, had orchestrated the "show" of the children's rescue to draw attention away from Dávila's death.

Colombians are well versed in brazen political scandals and their cover-ups. It's a country where popular presidents have turned out to be funded by drug cartels, where much-vaunted businesses have been revealed to be money-laundering machines, and where the army's supposed victories against guerrilla insurgents were exposed as the cold-blooded murder of civilians. Even in the niche genre of survival stories, there was a precedent. In 1955, the Colombian media heralded the miraculous tale of a sailor who had survived ten days in the Caribbean Sea after he was swept overboard from a navy destroyer. It took a young journalist by the name of Gabriel García Márquez to get to the truth. There had been no storm, as the navy had claimed—instead, the ship had been stacked high with smuggled goods that had come loose and dragged the sailor and seven of his companions into the waves.

History, therefore, had taught Colombians to be skeptical of good news, and there was an almost reflexive instinct to presume that darker currents—be they cartels, guerrillas, or shady political deals—flowed beneath the surface of the children's rescue story.

Now the details of Operation Hope became the subject of closer scrutiny. The retracted announcement of the children's rescue on May 15 was revisited. At the time, it had been dismissed as a simple case of confusion mixed with over-enthusiasm, born from a desire to deliver good news to the public: the rumor that had emerged around Cachiporro had been amplified by the president on social media without cross-checking the facts. Now, some began to question whether there had been truth to the rumor after all. Had the children been found and removed from the search area by boat? Why else would the huge search party, bolstered by sniffer dogs and advanced technology, have been unable to locate the children less than three kilometers from the crash site? Had an unsuspecting witness spotted the children on the lancha and reported the sighting over the radio?

This theory—that the children had been found in May but only "rescued" at a politically convenient moment for the government—stretched credibility and was soon put to bed. On June 21, the coroner ruled Oscar Dávila's death a suicide. The key evidence was traces of blood splatters on the sleeve of the deceased's right hand. In contrast to some neighboring countries, Colombia's institutions have maintained a reputation for independence and professionalism, and the report firmly undermined the notion that Operation Hope had been a smokescreen for a murder. But the now-debunked theory had had one thing going for it: it provided an explanation for how the children, including an eleven-month-old baby, had stayed alive for forty days. They had been given food and shelter by third parties.

On the first day of July, Salud Hernández-Mora, a journalist for *Semana* magazine, published a story that claimed to confirm what many Colombians had secretly suspected all along. It was headlined "The Children of the Jungle Were with the FARC."

CHAPTER TWENTY

Whispers

It was in San José del Guaviare that the rumors were most prevalent. The town of squat houses was once on the fringe of the Colombian Amazon, serving as a trading post for traffickers in animal pelts and rare wildlife. But in the 1980s and 1990s, the jungle was burned down to make way for coca plantations and, until the early 2000s, San José del Guaviare was firmly under control of the FARC. When I visited in November 2023, the town was enjoying a moment of relative prosperity. The central plaza, with its huge ceiba trees and its monument to the founding colonists, had been renovated. Alongside the plaza was a shopping mall and a cinema, and local travel agencies offered trips to waterfalls and ancient cave-painting sites for a growing tourism industry. But the long-term residents insisted that I not be taken in by the impression of normality. The guerrillas were still highly active in the region, they said, and they had their hands in everything—including the case of the children in the crashed plane.

In one of the town's tiny yellow taxis, the driver told me that the EMC was at war with another guerrilla group for the region's cocaine routes. With typical cabbie confidence, he explained how Ivan Mordisco's men had captured the lost children and used them to pressure the government to focus military attacks on their rivals. It was the sort of secret knowledge that the confession booth-like set-up of his workplace gave him access to. But it was hearsay. Later, a local journalist told me she had received a phone call in mid-May from a man who claimed to have seen the children in an Indigenous village on a tributary of the Apaporis. But he didn't leave a number, and the call hadn't been recorded. A local woman said she had sent children's clothes in an aid package and then had been shocked to see Lesly wearing them on the day of her rescue. At least, the jeans and blouse looked very similar in the photos that the army published. Finally, a resident who did not wish to be named told me he'd overheard a guerrilla boasting that his colleagues had held the children. But the guerrilla lived in the jungle and, even if he were contactable, he certainly wouldn't speak to a journalist

In her July article, Salud Hernández-Mora said that, having visited the region and traveled on the Apaporis's waters, she believed that the children had been found by members of Mordisco's EMC just a few days after crash-landing in the jungle. They were an opportunistic acquisition, one that could be used for political leverage, so the guerrillas removed them from the search area. The children were later found malnourished, she argued, because the guerrillas had lacked the supplies to feed them. The Apaporis—their only supply route—was under constant air surveillance. Only when the guerrillas felt safe and the flyovers slowed in frequency did they lead the children back to their eventual rescue point. Hernández-Mora said that her story was backed by sources who could not be revealed out of fear for their safety.

The article divided opinion. Online comments lauded Hernández-Mora's journalistic courage, while others criticized her for not giving sufficient recognition to the children's ability to feed themselves and to survive in the jungle. They pointed to similar cases of unlikely survival. In June 2015, five Indigenous girls between the ages of ten and fourteen had been found alive after nearly three weeks in the jungle when they'd got lost coming home from school in Vaupes. In 2020, a forty-year-old mother and her three children spent thirty-seven days wandering close to the Putumayo River, surviving on only seeds and water.

Other aspects of the *Semana* article didn't match facts on the ground. The military reported that the most up-to-date intelligence suggested the guerrillas were not operating in the region. On the jungle floor, aside from a long-abandoned camp, the commandos and expert Indigenous trackers had found no evidence of other groups in the forest—not even a footprint. The location of the children's eventual discovery by the Indigenous search party also didn't make sense under this theory. If the guerrillas had captured the children, the fastest, most viable way to extract them from the search area would have been via the Apaporis. The logical place to hold them would have been at a site to the east of the river, beyond the range of the soldiers and aerial reconnaissance. Under this scenario, the easiest and least risky way to return the children to the search area for "discovery" by rescuers would have been for the guerrillas to cross the river and leave them close to its west bank. But the children were found several kilometers into the jungle to the west—a trip that would have meant the guerrillas entering the heart of the search area and having to evade hundreds of soldiers.

Then there was the question of motive. The guerrillas denied having had the children, and it was not clear what they would have stood to gain by holding them. If they had encountered them in those first days, it would have been far simpler to announce the spectacular news, return them safely, and boost their own image with the public. If there was any political capital to be gained in keeping them, it wasn't evident in the months that followed, as the government hardened its approach to the EMC.

Finally, if it was a cover-up or a false-flag operation, it was an excessively expensive and loose one. The military inserted far more men than was typical for a rescue operation, and the decision to bolster their forces with hundreds of volunteers would have only served to create more potential witnesses to any nefarious activity. In the weeks that followed, journalists were given open access to commanders, troops, and Indigenous alike. None of the men who had been on the ground during the forty-day search operation indicated to me that they believed anyone else had ever had possession of the children. Even Manuel, who was no friend of the guerrillas and had defied them in the past, did not believe that they were involved. Hernández-Mora's article, he told me, was disrespectful. "The people who were there know it didn't happen that way," he says. "If the guerrillas had had the children, they would have asked for however many million [in ransom money], and they would never have delivered them so malnourished."

In San José del Guaviare, I tried to follow up with each lead regarding guerrilla involvement, but they all led to dead ends. I could find no evidence, and I could reach no authoritative source. It seemed most likely to me that, in a town where the memory of FARC control was still fresh, rumors and gossip exaggerated the guerrillas' influence and reach. If third-party involvement was to be ruled out, however, I needed to account for the most remarkable aspect of the children's story: Cristin's survival.

Narciso's explanation that the children had survived on fariña and fruit may have sufficed in the days after the rescue, but it seemed flimsier when no further details were forthcoming. The baby's bottle in which Lesly had supposedly mixed fariña with water had been found by Montiel's team on May 16—meaning that Cristin had survived for almost a month without it. The Indigenous often explained to incredulous journalists that the Western mind understood little of how Uitoto children are raised in the jungle, how they are schooled in its plants and animals from an early age. Where the white man sees the "green hell" of the *Vortex*, the Indigenous see all the resources they need to live on.

However, this didn't align with the experiences of the Uitoto, Muinane, and Andoke search parties. They told me of a barren, hostile jungle, with none of the abundant fruits of the Caquetá-Putumayo basin. If these experienced trackers and hunters had gone hungry around the banks of the Apaporis, how could four children be expected to survive forty days in the same territory? Part of the answer to this question was obvious: the children required fewer calories. They were smaller and burned less energy than the men on their incessant march. Still, I remained skeptical that the children, particularly Cristin, could find adequate nutrition for such an extended period. In my interviews, I confirmed that Herman had flown with a sizeable bag of fariña and that Magdalena often travelled with fruit for the children. I was also told, by someone who spoke to Lesly after the rescue, that Cristin's diaper bag had held sachets of powdered milk. But even that sounded like scant provisions for forty days.

It took a trip to La Chorrera to convince me that it was possible for the children to have sustained themselves for over a month. On a November afternoon I had sat in the town's central maloca, listening to long, mambé-fueled speeches from the tribal elders. The air under the palm-thatch roof was hot and humid, and when I stepped outside to cool off, the first drops of rain were falling. In the distance there was a streak of lightning, and soon the maloca shook under a boom of thunder. I took shelter under a nearby tree where a couple of Uitoto women were bent over a plastic bucket. Inside the bucket, the water was milky brown, and the plum-colored skins of milpeso fruits were floating on the surface as the women kneaded the flesh with their bare hands. When I asked, the two women were effusive about the super-juice they were preparing. It was better than milk from a mother's breast, said one. There was little doubt among the Uitoto that this small purple fruit had been the key to the children's survival. After all, the Indigenous rescue team had found Lesly with a milpeso seed in her cheek. In the unforgiving soils of the Apaporis grew the one Amazon plant capable of nourishing an eleven-month-old infant.

In May 2024, Aerocivil published a summary of an interview Lesly had given to its investigators to help understand the cause of the crash. She confirmed that the milpeso had been the children's primary source of food. There was no mention of the fariña or the powdered milk, but that was possibly a simple oversight. Lesly also provided a description of the events immediately preceding and following the crash of HK-2803 that helped to explain her actions and motivations. They tallied with what she had told her family in hospital.

The interview also added new, hitherto unknown elements to the children's account. In the maps of the search area the military had published to date, the path its analysts believed the children had taken was depicted in a luminous yellow line. It went west from the crash site to where the baby's bottle was found, then tacked northwards before doubling back to the south. There was no line headed east to the Apaporis, where Lesly told investigators she had caught a fish with a spiked stick. There seemed little reason to doubt this first-hand account. Lesly had heard the pilot say he was headed for a river and she had seen the Apaporis through the windshield, she explained. She knew that the most likely place to find a settlement was by the riverside, so it was logical that she would head in the direction that the plane had been traveling. True, the search teams had found no footprints or other evidence of the children between the Cessna and the river, but the military's GPS tracking map shows that this area was less well-explored than those to the west and north. They could easily have missed them.

However, some elements of the account published by the civil aviation authority were more confusing. Lesly said that she had found her way back to the Cessna after three days of aimless walking. That was a remarkable stroke of luck—given the difficulty that the soldiers had in locating the aircraft during their first week in the jungle—but not impossible. Stranger still was her explanation as to why the children had not approached the soldiers. Lesly said that she had heard people calling her name, but that she was worried the sounds could have been caused by predatory animals. That appeared to contradict the version she told her grandfather, in which she said she had deliberately hidden under a tree trunk and had muffled Cristin's cries with her hand. The GPS data also showed that the soldiers had patrolled right by the children's ultimate point of rescue on multiple occasions; close enough, surely, for the children to have been able to see them. It seems most likely to me that Lesly did indeed hide, although her motives—either because she thought they were guerrillas or because she feared punishment, as Narciso attested—are unclear.

No subject, however, fueled emotions and arguments more than that about Wilson. According to Pedro Sánchez, Lesly told him that a skinny dog was with the children in the days before their rescue. Narciso confirmed this version of events in his chat with the reporters at the hospital. On two separate occasions, Soleiny told her aunt Rosamira that the dog had chased away a pack of perros del monte. But on June 16, at a press conference called by OPIAC, Magdalena's brother was adamant that the children had never seen the dog. The Aerocivil report was equally categorical, stating that "there was no encounter with other people during their journey nor did they have contact with any canine."

The report did provide a valuable resource for anyone trying to understand the children's time in the jungle. As I tried to piece together the most probable version of events, I cross-referenced it with the family's accounts and other available information. If some of it was confused or contradictory, I reasoned, that was understandable, given the children's endless hungry days and cold, wet nights in a disorientating environment.

But one final element of the report concerned me. Lesly, it said, "had judiciously counted the days that passed since the accident … [facilitating] the investigation to put in chronology the aspects of their survival." Among other dates, she could pinpoint which days she heard aircraft in the jungle (days 10 to 15), when her foot stopped hurting (day 20), and the day she found the flier (day 30). That sounded unlikely to me. It was as if two versions of Lesly were being presented. One was a child whose ancestral culture enabled her to find food in the most hostile jungle, but also led her to believe that the soldiers' voices could belong to animals. The other was of a rational and careful planner, meticulously taking mental notes of dates and events, long past the point that most people would have lost their minds. It gave me the uneasy feeling that the interview Lesly gave to Aerocivil was, in some way, coached.

If the children hadn't seen a dog, why had they drawn one? This was not a trivial question. Why did Lesly tell General Sánchez that she had only picked fruits from the ground, but insisted to her grandmother that she had climbed trees to pluck them? Does a nine-year-old Indigenous girl draw the Colombian flag in the jungle without prompting from a patriotic adult? Physically weak and overawed by the attention they were receiving, it seemed that the children were either having words put in their mouths or were highly suggestible in response to the people who visited them.

To question the veracity of these accounts is not to diminish the resourcefulness, the mental fortitude, and the bravery shown by the children in the jungle. Nor is it to cast into question the crucial role that their Uitoto culture played in their survival. Given a sufficient supply of milpeso fruits, the children could have sustained themselves alone until the day of their rescue. But the differences between the version of events relayed to relatives at the hospital and the rather-too-neat report given to Aerocivil's investigators led me to suspect that the latter was strongly influenced by the adults who had visited the children during their stay in a children's home in the last six months of 2023.

Yet few people paid much attention to the inconsistencies contained in the Aerocivil report when it was released. By that time, Colombians were losing their appetite for a story that had left a sour taste. In Colombia, the worlds of *Encanto* and *Narcos* are deeply intertwined: the magical world frequently collides with a grim reality. On August 11, 2023, Manuel Ranoque was arrested in a park in northern Bogotá and taken to the prosecutor's office.

He was accused of the rape of Lesly Jacobombaire.

CHAPTER TWENTY-ONE

The Fight

Throughout Operation Hope, Manuel Ranoque's unwavering commitment to the search and his readiness to speak to the media made him a minor celebrity and a hero to Colombians. But in the days after the rescue, his mouth started to get him into trouble. On June 11, dressed in ripped jeans and a woolen sweater to ward off the Bogotá cold, he told reporters outside the military hospital that he had spoken to Lesly. "The only thing that [she] told me was that her mother was alive for four days," he said. "Before dying, their mother told them, 'Leave here, you are going to see who your father is, he knows what a father's love is, he has already demonstrated it to you.'"

In retrospect, this was an unlikely and self-serving statement; but in the days following the rescue, the world's media was hungry for any news about the children's ordeal, and many of them ran with the quote. It added another level of tragedy to the story. Magdalena, trapped in the plane, had been forced to send the children away, prioritizing their survival over her own. However, Manuel's version of events, according to which Magdalena used her final words to praise his own fatherly qualities, was the final straw in a family conflict that had been simmering under the surface.

The following day, Narciso Mucutuy spoke after visiting Lesly at the hospital. Lesly had told him, he said, that her mother and the other adults on board had died from the impact of the crash. This version of events was subsequently backed up by the Aerocivil's provisional report, which said that the three adult occupants had died from "multiple serious injuries, organ failure and severe bleeding." Two days later, Fatima spoke to Caracol Radio. "Lesly wanted nothing to do with [Manuel]. In fact, she wanted to die because he mistreated her mother so badly," she said. "The truth is he tried to abuse Lesly. He took her [into the jungle] and grabbed her, but she escaped from his hands. She came running and told her mother that he came up behind her and beat her. He was very abusive." The children's maternal grandparents said they would fight for custody of the four children.

The ICBF announced that the children would remain in their custody for six months while their rights were restored—a standard process for vulnerable children. While a team of psychologists began to make their assessments, Manuel was banned from visiting Lesly and Soleiny in the hospital.

A month after Manuel's arrest, the prosecutor's office published a document outlining the accusations against him. The abuse had started when Lesly was just ten years old, it said, and had been going on for three years. "He took advantage of the moments when he found himself alone with the minor, when the mother was working on the chagra and the other children weren't at home, in order to perform diverse and abusive sexual acts of carnal access." The document listed the alleged acts, which ranged from kissing and groping to multiple instances of rape. The investigation alleged that Manuel had told Lesly that, when she grew up, they would be married. When she tried to tell a family member of the abuse, he threatened her with a machete.

According to their interviews with Lesly, he had told her that if she continued to tell people, "He would kill her and feed her to the vultures."

In November 2023, I took the boat upstream from Araracuara to Puerto Sábalo in the company of Ismael Mendoza, Herman's eighty-three-year-old father. Reaching the village where Magdalena and her family had lived for four years before the accident had been no simple task. Following a twelve-hour bus ride from Bogotá to San José del Guaviare, we'd flown to Araracuara in an Antonov cargo plane loaded with construction materials, household appliances, and crates of Aguila beer. When we got to the dock in Puerto Arturo, Ismael negotiated with a boatman to take us three hours upriver, through the gorges and rapids, to Puerto Sábalo.

Logistics aside, the main challenge was security. Upriver from Araracuara, the EMC remained the de facto rulers of the territory. The arrival of any foreign visitor would not go unnoticed by the group's informants in town. Two months earlier, a foreign TV crew had been denied entry, but by the time of my visit the security situation on this stretch of the Caquetá had improved. In October, the Colombian military had announced the death of El Gato, the guerrilla accused of having killed four Indigenous children in May. The army said he had been killed in a firefight, but the EMC accused the soldiers of executing El Gato after his capture. In his camp, they had found firearms, hand grenades, and a fifteen-year-old Indigenous girl whom he had recruited and made his sexual partner. Two weeks later, the government announced a three-month ceasefire with the EMC, and opened peace talks with the guerrillas. In her smoky kitchen by the riverbank, an old Uitoto woman said that region felt safer, but she was still too cautious to give her name. Instead, she offered us each a glass of pineapple juice and the smoked vertebrae of a tapir, before bidding us farewell.

Ismael made quick work of the tapir, tearing flesh from bone with his teeth. I had been advised not to visit the monte upriver of Araracuara without an experienced and well-connected guide. Ismael fit the bill perfectly, and provided engaging company. We had met several times prior to the trip in Bogotá, where he had given me the impression of a shy man, small and frail under the many jackets and shirts he wore against the Andean air. But the jungle seemed to reinvigorate him. He powered up and down the tupui at Araracuara. On the river, he jumped from the canoe to muddy riverbanks to lash ropes with a boyish enthusiasm. As we went, he pointed out the old installations of the Araracuara penal colony that he remembered from his days as a prison guard— brick buildings covered in vines, former cattle ranches returned to trees, and the rusted machinery of an old timber mill looking like a steam engine lost in the jungle.

However, in the evenings, as we lay shirtless against the heat in hammocks that swung under the stilt houses, he seemed to despair. As a young man, he had resented the way his white bosses and the prisoners had treated him. But in the colony's absence, the runway and the road that served Araracuara had deteriorated to a pathetic degree.

For the People of the Center who inhabited the region, paying jobs only abound in the worlds of illegal logging, goldmining, and drug muling. He was skeptical that carbon bonds, the latest bonanza, would bring real benefits to the community. He worried about the security situation on the river, and recalled that it had been a threat from the FARC that had forced him to leave the community for good. As the sound of reggaeton drifted in from a nearby bar, Ismael, a practicing Catholic who had steered clear of the bottle most of his life, lamented the level of alcoholism in the community and the decline of the Indigenous culture he remembered from his youth. And now his eldest son, Herman, who had fought to arrest these changes, who had used his Bogotá education to fight for Indigenous rights, was gone.

When we reached Puerto Sábalo, the maloca where Lesly and her siblings had lived was abandoned, the corrugated-iron walls had been stripped away, and there was little sign that it had once housed a family. The chagra that Magdalena once tended still flourished, however, and grew thick with manioc plants. William Castro, once Manuel Ranoque's right-hand man, invited us to his house. When he was done telling us about Manuel and Magdalena's early years in Puerto Sábalo, he recounted the events of early April 2023.

"The problems began before the business with the carbon bonds," he said. In early 2023, having recently been elected governor, Manuel was sent to Bogotá to try to formalize Puerto Sábalo's legal recognition before the Colombian state. The community needed a tax number and a bank account, and it had to update its census data. He was given 6 million pesos, around US\$1,500, from the community budget for his expenses.

A few days after his arrival in the capital, he sent word back that these funds were insufficient, and a further 5 million pesos were arranged for him. Even with the extra resources, Manuel failed to complete his tasks. He said he'd been robbed of the money. But other paisanos in the city told William that Manuel had been spotted drinking and partying most nights. Fatima had also been in Bogotá during this time, and had seen Manuel and an ex-girlfriend of his eating dinner together in a hotel restaurant.

When Manuel returned to Puerto Sábalo, he was accompanied by the ex-girlfriend. William was furious, both with the waste of money and the manner of his arrival. "I told him he'd fucked everything up," he said. "I had a lot of trust in him ... but now he was arrogant and boastful."

The ex stayed for a week in Manuel's father's house, but Manuel told William and anyone who would listen that he planned to live under one roof with two girlfriends. He told the local boys that this was how a real man lived, much to Magdalena's humiliation. It wasn't, however, how the rest of the Catholic community lived. And while they might enjoy a party every few months to celebrate a wedding or a holiday, they were not accustomed to the daily drinking and loud music coming from Manuel's maloca.

"They would start drinking, turn to arguing, and then end up fighting outside," William said. He gave Manuel three days to send his ex on her way, but they ignored the ultimatum. One of Magdalena's brothers arrived with a rifle to threaten Manuel, but he escaped. When Magdalena wouldn't accept the living conditions that Manuel wanted to impose on her, he became physically violent. She took to bathing in the river in the early morning to hide the bruises, but she was soon confronted by the women of the village, and told them of the abuse. As local feeling soured towards him, Manuel talked about moving away with Magdalena. "I told both of them, 'It doesn't matter where you live, unless you change you will find the same problems wherever you go—it doesn't matter if it's Bogotá, Switzerland, or the United States,'" William said.

One night in early April, the villagers heard screams coming from the maloca. Manuel was beating Magdalena with the flat side of a machete. Photos taken the next day showed her back and neck covered in deep-purple bruises. William says that Manuel also beat the children. As the couple yelled at each other, their neighbors heard a chilling accusation: Magdalena shouted that Manuel had tried to abuse Lesly. William's version of events coincided with the account that Fatima Mucutuy had given to the press in the days after the rescue.

The community was furious with Manuel, and William was forced to act. He knew that Manuel had a history of violence and drug use, and that this latest disturbance would attract the attention of the guerrillas, who would most likely demand swift justice.

William called an emergency meeting of the community, and they voted to revoke Manuel's governorship. They also decided on his punishment. Article 246 of Colombia's constitution allows Indigenous people to apply their own laws in their territories. The Nasa people of south-western Colombia punish drug offenses with a set of lashes to the calves of the perpetrator, followed by the application of a healing water containing sacred plants to signify their return to the community. For serious crimes, the Ticunas of the Amazon can sentence the guilty party to be tied to a tree and exposed to the fiery bites of giant ants. Other punishments are symbolic. For the Amazonian Kichwa people, who inhabit the border region of Colombia and Ecuador, long hair is a symbol of knowledge and synonymous with respect, so cutting a Kichwa's locks is a humiliating gesture and considered a severe punishment.

In Puerto Sábalo, the elders chewed on their mambé and decided that Manuel needed to purge his body and soul of his destructive ways. To do so would require the ingestion of 200 grams of ambil in liquid form, a dose that would either expel the evil within or, quite possibly, prove fatal.

"The purge can cure someone both morally and psychologically—a new person can be born," says William. Even so, the use of such quantities of ambil was not a common recourse; the elders could remember only one other time they had used the punishment. Manuel, who was no fan of traditional medicines, and who two months later would react badly to the yagé offered by Don Rubio, decided not to take any chances. When he got wind of the punishment, he disappeared, taking a lancha in the night.

In William's version of events, there had been no threat to Manuel from the EMC. He had been ousted by the villagers, who could no longer turn a blind eye to his abuse.

"What they say Magdalena endured is a reflection of the reality for many women in the jungle," says Maria Kuiru, the female governor of one of La Chorrera's communities, who prefers to go by her Indigenous name, Jitomakury. I met her at the side of the airstrip in La Chorrera, where she wore jeans and sneakers and a straw hat against the midday sun. She was patient with my questions, even when the answers were frustrating or painful for her. For over thirty years, she has been fighting to provide better protection for women and children in the Amazon.

Uitoto society had always been patriarchal, and her own father had been no different. Fate, however, had blessed him with eight daughters, all of them possessing a rebellious streak, in Jitomakury's telling. As a teenager, she took up smoking—not because she liked the taste, but because the men of the village told her she couldn't. At the age of twenty, she became the first female governor in La Chorrera. The other twenty male governors regarded her as a curious oddity.

But Jitomakury was a pioneer. Today, there are eight female governors of La Chorrera's twent- two communities. Since the late 1980s, national policy and cultural change have eroded some of the community's more patriarchal practices. "Women took the reins, we got stronger, we began to demand our rights," she says. The once-common practice of arranged marriage between clans was largely eliminated, and new laws regarding the age of sexual consent helped reduce the practice of marrying off girls as soon as they begin menstruating. In La Chorrera, an ICBF post was introduced and a legal pathway opened for the prosecution of gender-based violence.

Despite these advances, in the last five years the municipality of La Chorrera has had some of the highest rates of domestic and sexual abuse in Colombia. Too often, says Jitomakury, cases of domestic abuse or rape are settled between families, with the culprit paying some form of compensation. Children, left at home while their mothers work in the chagra or housed in the region's boarding schools, far from their parents' communities, are particularly vulnerable. Often, the abuse is perpetrated by a family member. In one case, she says, a woman knew that her husband had been raping their daughters, but said nothing out of fear. There have also been dozens of cases of child sex abuse perpetrated by public functionaries—including teachers, priests, and soldiers—in the region around La Chorrera. Without a police presence, many more cases go unreported, according to a former public prosecutor for the region who in 2020 decried the systematic state abandonment and pact of silence in the communities.

It didn't use to be this way. Uitoto culture, with its focus on life and abundance, valued the life-giving properties of women, and held them in reverence. In nearly every case of domestic or sexual abuse that Jitomakury has witnessed in the community, alcohol or other drugs have been involved. "We are seeing a loss of our culture," she says. "We've taken strong blows from the Western world—first with the rubber trade, then with the boom for animal pelts, and now for coca. They brought with them alcohol, loud music, and a desire for luxury goods, creating the conditions for this kind of abuse."

On a remote stretch of the Caquetá River, Magdalena and her children were even more vulnerable than they were in La Chorrera. Not only was there no ICBF presence, but the army and the police didn't dare set foot in Puerto Sábalo. The only recourse was the community, but there was a very high bar for intervention. Families tended to mind their own business, according to William Castro; and, besides, Manuel had already established sufficient authority in the community to be appointed governor. Where could she turn?

The day after that final fight, Magdalena left Puerto Sábalo. That morning, Lesly, Soleiny, and Tien were nowhere to be found. "She took [Cristin], she searched for the children, but couldn't find them," says William Castro. "She was trying to wake up from this nightmare, to forget what had happened. She was very, very hurt, but she was strong." Eventually, she gave up looking. Her brother arrived in a lancha to ferry her and Cristin to Chukiki.

This could and perhaps should have been the end of the story. Manuel could have lived out his life in Bogotá, as one of the millions of Colombians forced to leave their rural communities. Magdalena and her family could have stayed on in Puerto Sábalo or Chukiki, safe from their abuser.

During her stay in Chukiki, family members say they saw Magdalena talking animatedly on the phone. At some point, she apparently made the decision to go along with Manuel's plan to leave Puerto Sábalo for Bogotá. The motivations for her decision, given the abuse she had suffered and her knowledge of the threat that Manuel posed to Lesly, are hard to untangle. William says that the villagers of Puerto Sábalo had reached the conclusion that she was a masochist. Fidencio Mucutuy, Magdalena's uncle, says that Manuel had "brainwashed" her with promises of a house and money in the capital. The family tried to prevent her leaving. It was he, Fidencio told local news in July 2023, who had called the operator of the cargo flights to request that they deny Magdalena boarding.

Magdalena, however, could not be swayed. In Araracuara, she tried in vain to board the cargo flights, and continued to communicate with Manuel to pressure the police to prioritize their safe passage to escape the threat from the guerrillas. It is not certain, however, that Magdalena planned to travel to Bogotá or to live with Manuel. Some of the Uitoto, such as her childhood friend Diana Rodriguez, speculate that she might never have planned to take the bus to Bogotá, but to stay in San José del Guaviare at the house of a relative. She could have escaped the jungle and Manuel in one go. Her true motives may never be known.

On the night that Manuel attacked Magdalena, Lesly gathered Soleiny and Tien, and took them away from the house. She led them along the thin dirt path that wound through the chagra, and helped them traverse the narrow planks that bridged the streams. They walked up the hill, past the soccer pitch and the tiny school that sat on the crest in an open field, overlooking the village below. They kept going. Lesly led them into the dark of the monte, where the canopy swallowed up the last light of the stars. There she made a shelter from the palm leaves, and pulled her siblings close.

In November 2023, I retraced this route, guided by one of Lesly's friends. He scanned the forest on each side of the path and named the fruits they gave. *Canangucho, camu camu, juan soco, milpesos.* He told me that Lesly and her siblings would often disappear during the heated, alcohol-fueled arguments between Manuel and Magdalena. Sometimes, the children returned the same evening, when the shouting had died down. Other times, they came back the next morning. This time, they stayed in the jungle for three days before they returned to Puerto Sábalo and were eventually reunited with Magdalena and Cristin in Chukiki. During this time, Lesly fed her siblings with the fruits and seeds of the trees, the ones she had learned about from her mother.

CHAPTER TWENTY-TWO

Custody

On July 14, 2023, having spent just over a month in the military hospital, the four children were moved to an ICBF children's home on the northern outskirts of Bogotá. It was a friendly and spacious facility, home to sixty other children. The playrooms and accommodation were dispersed amongst large gardens, and the pointy roofs helped give the impression of a traditional Indigenous village. The ICBF went to unusual lengths to ensure that the children felt comfortable. Uitoto carers were hired to speak to the children in their native language. A small chagra was set up for the residents to sow and harvest plants. Visitors brought the children their favorite foods—fariña, smoked fish, and jungle fruits—and their companions in the home soon became familiar with the rich odors of Amazonian cooking.

Tien's appetite, on such occasions, was a source of astonishment to his carers. The first to finish his plate, and quick to ask for seconds, the five-year-old often had to be reminded of the virtues of sharing, but his boisterous energy and mischievous streak elicited more chuckles than scoldings. General Pedro Sánchez recalls a moment of brief panic on one of his regular visits to the children when he thought he had misplaced his commando beret. It soon reappeared, hanging low on Tien's brow as he marched around, one hand raised in salute, chanting, "I'm the general!"

Soleiny, too, was quick to settle in. Talkative and outgoing, she quickly made friends with the other children, and spent a lot of time playing and helping the younger ones. Lesly, however, remained quiet and aloof. She preferred to spend her time painting and, in the first months at least, interacted less with the other children. She suffered recurrent nightmares, often involving her mother's death. But while each child reacted differently to their time in the ICBF home, they shared a common desire: all three wanted to return to Uitoto territory.

Under the ICBF's guidelines, when a child is deemed to be at risk of violence or mistreatment, and if they don't have a home environment that can keep them safe, a process of "re-establishment of rights" must be undertaken. Initially, at least, the organization said its preference was to house the children together. This seemed to favor the case for custody to be awarded to Fatima and Narciso as maternal grandparents to all four. Given the serious and credible allegations against him, Manuel Ranoque was no longer considered an option, but his sister in Puerto Sábalo had stepped in to petition for custody of Tien and Cristin. Meanwhile, Andrés Jacobombaire wanted Lesly and Soleiny to return to his household. He pointed out that they had two full siblings, Angie and John Andrés, who still lived in La Chorrera—a factor seemingly overlooked in the ICBF's preferred course of action.

Throughout the search for his daughters, Andrés had stayed out of the limelight. His frail state had made it impossible for him to join the search team, and he had listened with frustration to Manuel Ranoque's interviews on TV and radio. Not only had Manuel done nothing to correct reports that he was the father of all four children, but he seemed to promote the idea. In the early days of the search, when the family members waited for news in the aircraft hangar in Villavicencio, Manuel had introduced himself as Magdalena's husband. This wasn't true, as Andrés and Magdalena had never divorced. In the Avianline offices, Rosamira says she confronted Manuel after hearing that he had taken to signing Lesly and Soleiny's surname as Ranoque. During the argument, she says, Manuel claimed to possess civil registry papers naming him as the father of both girls. He never produced them, and all state documentation cited Andrés as the pair's father. Nevertheless, the Colombian public remained largely ignorant of the fact that the four children had two different fathers. When he first met Pedro Sánchez at Lesly's bedside, Andrés says, the general seemed surprised to hear that Andrés was her father.

After their first visit to the children's ward in the military hospital, Andrés, Rosamira, and Jairo returned during their visiting hours on the following two Sundays. They brought food and toys, and showed Lesly and Soleiny photos of the house in La Chorrera where they had spent their early years, and photos of Angie and John Andrés. They remembered their brother and sister, and, according to Andrés and Rosamira, said they wanted to return to La Chorrera. At this point, Andrés says, his thoughts were only on the wellbeing of his daughters, but on his final visit to the hospital, on June 31, he was invited for a coffee by the Mucutuy family.

Over the course of the previous two months, the two families had become closer as they shared the anxiety of the search, their grief over Magdalena's death, and their relief at the children's rescue. Andrés had held Narciso in high regard since his visit to Puerto Sábalo. Now, however, he was introduced to a lawyer who asked him to sign some papers that he said would guarantee that the children would not be held in ICBF custody. When Andrés refused to sign, he says, the man got angry. This marked the first steps of a protracted and continuing legal battle for custody of the children.

Rosamira had once cleaned the apartment of a lawyer in the north of the city, and now she turned to him for advice. Fredy Quintero has thinning hair, a cheerful demeanor, and none of the pomposity you find in Bogotá's big legal firms. We met several times over the course of late 2023 and early 2024, and each time he looked a little more baffled by the case's latest turn. His first move was a request to review the contract that Andrés had been asked to sign. When it failed to materialize, he concluded that it had been disadvantageous to his client. No matter, he thought, the law was clear: in the event of a parent's death, the surviving parent has the right of custody. At Rosamira's request, he agreed to represent Andrés.

"I thought it would be straightforward, regular custody case," he told me, "but I soon got the impression that the ICBF were determined to undermine Andrés' case for custody." The initial problems seemed to be ones of omission, he said. When the children were discharged from hospital, Andrés was not informed. On July 6, President Petro hosted a meeting at the Casa de Nariño, the neoclassical presidential palace in downtown Bogotá. In attendance were Astrid Cáceres, the head of the ICBF, and Fatima and Narciso Mucutuy. Afterwards, Cáceres told the press that the government would set up a fund to secure the economic future of the children, and that it had been a "friendly meeting" in which "the family could raise the points they wanted with the president." But Andrés and his family had not been invited.

The task of finding a single home for the four children was complicated by the fact that the three older children had different preferences. From the very start, Soleiny had remained determined that she wanted to return to La Chorrera and to her older siblings. Lesly, however, appears to have changed her mind during her time in hospital. There is no disputing that Andrés visited his daughter three times in the hospital. Those meetings were, by his own account, happy ones, in which Lesly welcomed the chance to reconnect with the family. According to Andrés and Rosamira, during this time she said she wanted to return to her childhood home in La Chorrera.

At the children's home, however, Lesly's attitude changed. On the Jacobombaires' visits, Soleiny, happy and talkative as ever, would go over to hug her father and aunt. Meanwhile, Tien would sneak out of his lodgings to wrestle with Jairo, whom he had grown fond of and now called "Tio" (uncle). Lesly, however, remained in her dormitory. She was annoyed, someone who spoke with her during this time told me, that her father wanted to see her now, when he had never visited her during her six years in Puerto Sábalo.

Andrés was hurt by the accusation. He maintains that he tried repeatedly to persuade Magdalena to return his daughters to him during their estrangement. The fight for custody of the children turned bitter. Allegations, old and new, were made. Andrés accused the Mucutuys of turning his oldest daughter against him. Fatima accused Andrés of abusing Magdalena. Manuel claimed Fatima was a drunkard who had never cared much for her grandchildren prior to the crash.

At the first hearing, in December 2023, having worked on the case for six months, the ICBF could not advise the courts on who should be granted custody of the children, and extended the period needed for the re-establishment of rights for a further six months. In June 2024, it was extended again. In Colombia, it is common for child welfare cases to slip through the cracks, but in such a high-profile case the delay seemed inexplicable. By now, both the Jacobombaires and the Mucutuy families were united, at least, in their frustration with the glacial pace at which the ICBF appeared to moving. Surely a year was enough to assess the custody claims of each of the families? Even if neither of them met the requirements, a foster home could have been identified, allowing the children to return to some semblance of normal life.

What were the reasons for the delay? Why hadn't Andrés been awarded custody of Lesly and Soleiny at the first hearing? Why hadn't he been invited to the event at the Casa de Nariño? I put these questions to the ICBF, but no amount of follow-up elicited a response.

At the time of writing, the custody case is continuing, and the details are confidential. However, from my conversations with people who have knowledge of the case, I gained a broad idea of the nature of the accusations made between the different parties and their potential motives. The only judicious thing to say is that the custody battle provoked in me a sorrow for Lesly's predicament; I got the impression that now, after her ordeal in the jungle, she was being subjected to a different form of turmoil. My gut feeling was that she was now a pawn in a struggle between adults who wanted to influence the story she had to tell. This would potentially explain the inconsistencies between what she told her family in the hospital and the version she gave later to Aerocivil investigators. Who, apart from family members, had visited the children at the children's home? Again, the ICBF would not give me an answer.

The children's story was now worth a lot of money. In the week following the publication of my stories about their rescue in *The Guardian*, I received half a dozen emails from documentary filmmakers requesting help in gaining "access" to the children and their families. I tried to explain that the children were still weak, recovering in hospital, and likely traumatized from the events. It would be months, I assumed, before they would be able to talk about their ordeal.

Nevertheless, on June 22, while the children were still in hospital, Petro announced on X that Simon Chinn, a two-time Oscar winner, would team up with state broadcaster RCTV to make a documentary on Operation Hope and the children's time in the jungle. It is unclear on what legal basis the government or the TV company made this announcement. Under Colombian law, such decisions regarding children are the responsibility of their legal guardians. In the case of Lesly and Soleiny, that was Andrés. The *patria de potestad*, the right of parental authority, could only be removed from a parent in the case of abandonment or abuse. Andrés had not abandoned his daughters—they had been taken from him. In the second half of 2023, when other relatives of the children and members of the search team had accepted payments to appear on hastily produced documentaries, Andrés had turned down offers for public interviews.

It took until February 2024 for representatives from the presidentially endorsed documentary team to make their first contact with Quintero, having recognized Andrés as the oldest children's legal representative. Andrés told me that his dream was to secure the financial freedom for Lesly and Soleiny that would allow them to attend university and have the opportunity to travel and study abroad. The contract offered them that chance. The revenues from the film would be invested in a fund to benefit all four survivors of HK-2803, and would be managed by the ICBF and a local non-government organization.

In May 2024, Lesly and Soleiny gave filmed interviews for the documentary team. In August, Quintero helped them file paperwork to obtain their passports and visas for the United States. The film was due to be broadcast before the end of the year, when the children would likely still be in ICBF custody, but plans were being made to allow them to attend the premiere.

In June, the ICBF published an update on the children to mark the one-year anniversary of their rescue. A photo showed the four of them sitting together on a grassy verge, hands aloft and with bright smiles. The children were continuing their studies, the accompanying statement read, and were being attended to by a support team specializing in Indigenous rights who would ensure that they didn't lose touch with their customs, despite being far from home. "We should send a deep thanks to the Mucutuy siblings," it concluded, "given that they united all Colombians in a single cause."

But those who visited the children said they were bored and frustrated after a year in the Bogotá children's home. They wanted to return to their families.

Epilogue

A year after the rescue, the sterile interior of the CCOES's Bogotá office has been given a splash of color. In the ground-floor entrance hall, a giant map of the jungle search area covers the wall. A spider's web of yellow lines traces the routes that the soldiers patrolled over the course of five weeks, and an accompanying photo gallery features prowling commandos, stoic-faced Indigenous searchers, and the dramatic scenes of the children's helicopter rescue. In contrast to the trophy cabinet of guerrilla souvenirs ensconced on the third floor, the new installation is a prominent and wholesome endorsement of the military's most high-profile humanitarian mission.

By now, General Pedro Sánchez is well used to interviews. Over the past twelve months, he has become a regular face in the Colombian media, featuring in TV shows and at book fairs, and has become perhaps the most recognizable soldier in the country's recent history. It's been a sudden departure from the man who extolled the anonymous, shadowy work of his unit during our first meeting. His fame has raised eyebrows among some of the stuffier members of the officer's mess, but Sánchez brushes off any suggestion of careerism. If he has to leave the army tomorrow and milk cows, he says, then that's what he'll do.

It's clear, however, that he takes his public relations role seriously. When I ask him if he thinks Operation Hope has changed Colombian perceptions of the military, he has the relevant opinion polls at hand on his smartphone. Yes, there was a brief spike in the armed forces' approval ratings in mid-2023, but it has since fallen back, still well below support levels in the 2000s. He feels that the soldiers' role has been underplayed in media accounts of the operation. The Indigenous were vital members of the search team, but the successful rescue depended mostly on military strategy, technology, and logistics, he reminds me.

"There was distrust and confrontation," he says. "We'd say, 'Look at the map, look at the compass.' The Indigenous would take yagé and talk to the spirits." In the end, he says, the ability to work through this clash of cultures served only to prove something he already knew. "Unity is strength," he says, before reaching for a volume on a bookshelf stuffed with titles pertaining to leadership and self-improvement.

He chooses one called *The Power of Kaballah*, and thumbs his way to an underlined section. "There are two realities," he says. "The world of darkness is 1 per cent; the kingdom of light is 99 per cent." There are still aspects of the operation that he finds difficult to explain: the children's miraculous survival, the commandos' failure to locate them, and the role of yagé in their rescue. Knowledge is like water in a glass, he suspects. If it's full to the brim, there's no space for new learning. "You need to leave 1 per cent for the world of darkness," he says.

I get the feeling, however, that the books relating to stoicism might offer more consistent succor for his daily work. Leading the Colombian Special Forces can seem like a Sisyphean task. On the day that the children were rescued, CCOES troops were also taking part in a covert and unheralded operation to eliminate a high-profile drug trafficker. In October 2023, it was one of the commando teams that had patrolled the Apaporis in search of the children that managed to kill El Gato, the guerrilla accused of running the EMC's child recruitment. But by June 2024, after a broken ceasefire, the EMC had strengthened its control over large parts of southern Colombia, shooting up police stations and detonating roadside bombs in civilian populations. President Petro's plan to strike multiple peace deals with the country's myriad armed groups was in tatters. The commandos returned to their professional staple: the "catch-or-kills."

With so much money at stake for the control of the jungle's riverine drug routes, and with such little state capacity to police them, the death of one leader only results in the promotion of another. The weakening of one illegal armed group only emboldens the next. Sánchez gives the impression of being cut from a different cloth than many of his predecessors. Since his embrace of Giovani Yule, the Nasa leader, he has become a trusted figure for many Indigenous and has provided a glimmer of hope that military-civilian relations in the Amazon might improve. But the general is under no illusions about the dire security situation faced by the People of the Center, whose way of life is threatened by the encroachment of outsiders.

"It showed us a sad reality of the country," he says despairingly. "It's a reality in which the population has been abandoned to the mercy of illegal groups." He recognizes that many of the investments needed to provide better protection, access and state services to jungle communities could have unintended consequences for Indigenous culture or the environment. "There's so much poverty, but sometimes installing a new paved airstrip means that around the town the forest will be chopped down," he says. "It's a very difficult balance to strike. There's a people who want to move forward, but the illegal groups cling to them."

In December 2023, following pressure from Indigenous groups, the Aerocivil announced it would spend $750,000 on repaving the runway at Araracuara. The accompanying press release said that, in addition to improving landing and takeoff conditions, the investment would boost trade and tourism in the Amazon region.

But such investments are unlikely to be made as long as the security situation in Caquetá changes like the seasons. The relative calm in which I found the region in November 2023 turned out to be a brief respite in a worsening situation. In June 2024, I went to a dinner to celebrate Diana Mendoza's graduation from nursing school. This happy event, attended by dozens of members of Bogotá's Uitoto community, and well stocked with Johnnie Walker whiskey, was tinged with regret for those not present. On the wall, behind a three-tiered white cake, were two framed photos: one of Herman Mendoza, and the other of his mother, Ismael's wife, who had died in August 2022.

Delio Mendoza, looking slimmer now, and Ismael, dressed in a brown suit and tie, made moving tributes to Herman and the work he had dedicated his life to. Ismael was proud of Diana's achievement. It was a challenge, he said, for the Uitoto to overcome prejudices and to obtain their professional goals while still maintaining a connection with their culture. He only hoped that these opportunities could extend to the People of the Center in their home territory. A week after the dinner, the Mendoza family was struck by another tragedy: masked men gunned down one of Ismael's nephews in broad daylight in Araracuara.

The EMC had reasserted its authority over the Caquetá River.

A few months earlier, Manuel Ranoque's attorney, Sebastian Moreno, travelled to Puerto Sábalo in the company of Don Rubio. Before an assembly of the village elders, he requested that his client be tried locally under traditional Indigenous justice. In return, Manuel was prepared to return the funds he had taken from the carbon-bond project. The assembly rejected his petition. "They told me the guerrillas wouldn't allow it," he says.

The lawyer's fortunes then took a turn for the worse. While he was in Puerto Sábalo, the EMC announced an armed blockade of the Caquetá River, and he soon got word that the guerrillas were coming for him. Lying down in the hull of a lancha to avoid detection, Moreno and Rubio left in the dead of night and spent three days hiding out in a village downriver. Eventually, Moreno managed to escape detection and reach the airstrip at Araracuara, where he found a flight out on a cargo plane.

After spending three days talking to sources in Puerto Sábalo, Moreno concluded that Manuel had indeed been threatened by the guerrillas. "They told me they tied him to a tree and beat him," he says. "They asked the locals whether they should kill him or not." The guerrillas, he points out, do not take kindly to allegations of domestic and sexual abuse in the community. The EMC have denied threatening Manuel, and this account contradicts the story told to me by William Castro, but Moreno's version of events matches what I was told by other sources who spoke to me on the condition of anonymity.

Whether the guerrillas threatened to recruit Lesly, or whether, in fact, she sought to enter their ranks to escape her stepfather, I can't say. What is clear, however, is that thousands of children across Colombia's Amazon and other remote regions are highly vulnerable as a result of the presence of illegal armed groups and the absence of state control. Guerilla membership is not without its attractions. The jobs they provide in a range of illegal industries offer young Indigenous the rare opportunity to escape poverty and to provide for their families. The EMC's provision of food and financial assistance to the community during the Covid-19 pandemic also expanded their influence in regions the state had left behind. Finally, the swift and brutal justice they mete out to violent and volatile elements, such as Manuel Ranoque, provides a modicum of stability in an unpoliced region.

But all this comes at the price of obedience and silence. Over the course of my research, many of the Indigenous bemoaned the physical risks the armed groups posed to them and their families, the corruption that guerrilla money brought to local politics, and the rapid erosion of their culture brought about by access to drugs, weapons, and prostitution. For some, the only option is to leave their ancestral lands and move to the poorest neighborhoods of big cities, far from the family networks and culture of their people. This was the decision that Magdalena made when she decided to board her family on Cessna HK-2803.

The shadow of the violence cast by the armed groups is not the only risk to the vulnerable children of the Amazon. Sometimes, the threat is closer to home. When I last spoke to Manuel Ranoque, it was on a video call from his cell in a wing for sex offenders in a high-security Bogotá prison. He had been transferred there at his own request after an EMC member was incarcerated at his previous low-security jail. With regard to the ongoing legal case against him, he maintains his innocence. He says that Lesly and Soleiny were like his own daughters, and that his determination to search for them in the jungle was evidence of his devotion to them. Besides, he says, he was never alone with them. His days were spent ferrying marijuana, felling trees, and hunting, and Magdalena didn't take well to him hanging around the house.

Such testimony is unlikely to work in his favor. Aside from a history of false statements that he has made—including the assertion that Magdalena survived for four days after the crash— he is unlikely to find many witnesses for the defense in Puerto Sábalo, following his embezzlement of project funds and the alcohol-fueled disorder he brought to the community. More importantly, Lesly's testimony against him is damning and is backed up by medical evidence. Unless she retracts it, Manuel is likely to spend between fourteen and twenty years behind bars.

If the Cessna had never crashed in the jungle, Manuel's abuse of Lesly—if the courts confirm that is what took place—could have continued. If the children hadn't defied all the odds to survive until their rescue, it is unlikely that the case would have made it to court. How many similar cases go unpunished across the Amazon, and in Colombia's other remote regions, due to the expectation of impunity? The depressing reality, confirmed by my conversations with local activists and international organizations, is that rates of domestic and sexual abuse, already high, are likely to be significantly underreported. Even with more funding, it's hard to see how the ICBF could increase its coverage in remote Amazonian communities under the current security situation.

Most Colombians are familiar with—and exhausted by—the seemingly intractable challenges that confront their country. In a mestizo country, where the vast majority of inhabitants have some Indigenous blood in their veins, there was a surge of pride that Lesly, Soleiny, Tien, and Cristin had given the world an unprecedented example of the endurance of the human spirit and the importance of preserving ancient native knowledge. Lesly, in particular, was lauded as a national hero for her strength and maturity. The story intertwined nicely with Gustavo Petro's vision of Colombia as a "world power of life"—a message that will presumably be emphasized in the state-backed documentary of the children's story.

For that message to ring true, however, the country will have to arrest the rapid erosion of Indigenous culture. The belief systems of the Uitoto and the Amazon's many other tribes are part of what ethnobotanist Wade Davis has called "the ethnosphere," the sum total of all global beliefs and ideas since the existence of the human race. It is, in his view, "humanity's greatest legacy." In the same way that the biosphere is degraded by the loss of animal and plant systems, the ethnosphere is being eroded by the loss of world culture, albeit at a much faster rate. The knowledge of the forest—passed through generations—that empowered Lesly to save her siblings is under threat from extractive industries, new technology, and a powerful global culture. So, too, is the ancestral spirituality that helped the Indigenous teams find the children, as new generations eschew the teachings of their grandparents.

Men like Don Rubio are a dying breed. In the days following the rescue, he performed a cleansing ceremony on the men from Puerto Leguízamo who had found the children. All of them had flu-like symptoms, and two of them had leishmaniasis, but they soon returned to strength. There was no one with the knowledge to perform the ritual on Rubio himself, however. He'd left the jungle with a sore throat and a hoarse voice—the result, he said, of the duende grabbing him by the neck. In the coming months, his physical and mental condition deteriorated. He had ticks and lice from the jungle, and he could feel parasites within his body. Even worse, he said, his soul had absorbed dark energies from the jungle spirits and the duende. He felt himself going crazy, and then he fell into a depression. "I wanted to go back to the monte and drown in the river," he told me.

In April 2024, after returning from his perilous trip along the Caquetá River with Manuel's lawyer, Rubio decided to visit a friend's house in the jungle outside Puerto Leguízamo. There he took yagé for the first time since his stint in the Apaporis, carefully preparing the vine to bring about the purge he needed. It cleansed his body, but also brought him awareness and a new purpose. He thought of the two sons he had lost and the prospect of his disappearing heritage. "When I am fully recovered, I want to teach," he told me when we last spoke. He noted that more young men were starting to take mambé, and he could sense their yearning to learn more about their people's past and culture. "I want to set up a maloca where I can teach them to cure with plants, to sing, to take yagé, and to commune with the spirits."

Rubio was in high spirits, talkative and cheerful, a seemingly different man from the taciturn and mysterious figure he had cut in the jungle. And he had one final piece of good news: according to him, Wilson is alive and well. Rubio had bristled at accusations that, in his confrontation with the duende, he had used the search dog as a bargaining chip for the children's lives. Now, in the visions brought on by the yagé, he saw the Belgian shepherd walking in the jungle, accompanied by two men. They explained to him that Wilson had run off in pursuit of a perro del monte which had been in heat, but that they were now protecting him. "He's there in the Apaporis—the tigers haven't eaten him," says Rubio. "The dog is content."

Sadly, at the time of writing, Lesly, Soleiny, Tien, and Cristin do not have the liberty to return to the jungle. They remain in ICBF care, and their future is uncertain. There is a hope, or perhaps an expectation, among many Colombians that Lesly will become a symbol of Amazonian culture and the importance of ancestral knowledge, as a Greta Thunberg–type champion of Indigenous rights.

It remains to be seen whether Lesly, just fourteen years old, wants to assume such a role. Colombia has had Amazonian heroes in the past. In 1976, Alberto Lesmes Rojas—better known as Kapax—swam the 1,600-kilometer length of the Magdalena River over the course of five weeks. The "Tarzan of the Amazon" became an instant celebrity and a promoter of environmental causes in the Colombian Amazon. Now seventy-seven, he lives in a small house in the center of Leticia. In the years since his greatest feat, one million square kilometers of Amazon rainforest have been hacked away across South America.

For as long as Colombia has been a country, it has turned its back on the jungle and its people. Across the region, thousands of vulnerable children suffer the effects of state abandonment. Many more will be lost to the forest or recruited by illegal groups, will become victims of domestic abuse, or will succumb to alcoholism or drug addiction. But, despite these conditions, the People of the Center—even those displaced to the cities—feel a deep emotional connection to their clans and their jungle territories.

The last time Andrés visited Soleiny, he says, his youngest daughter began to cry. "I just want to go home," she said.

Acknowledgements

I began researching this book in Bogotá, 600 kilometers away from where its events took place and 2,000 meters closer to the sky. I had little experience of the Amazon jungle, and if I have been able to capture any of its essence on these pages, it is due to the generosity and patience of the Uitoto, Muinane, and Andoque men and women who helped me in the subsequent months. At a time when travel to Araracuara and the surrounding stretches of the Caquetá River seemed impossible, Ismael Mendoza proved an essential and entertaining guide. I will forever remember the long days on the river, the caguana and smoked tapir, and the hammock-bound conversations of that week. Thank you, Ismael.

I am also grateful to the Jacobombaire family for trusting me when I had little to offer save my curiosity about their story. During a difficult period, Andrés, Rosamira, and Jairo took the time to meet with me and help me understand the events that had shaped Magdalena's early life. In this regard, I must also extend my thanks to Diana Rodríguez for providing her unique perspective. Magdalena was lucky to count you as a friend.

I must also thank Edwin Paky for his detailed explanation of the Indigenous search efforts and Don Rubio for his colorful descriptions of the power of yagé and the face of the duende.

In Bogotá, General Pedro Sánchez was generous with his time, spending several afternoons discussing the finer points of military strategy and helping organize meetings with the soldiers and pilots who played such a central role in the rescue of the children.

Finally, I must thank all the paisanos, pilots, policemen, anthropologists, security experts, and historians who met with me during my research. Some have been quoted here, many have not, but none of them bears any responsibility for any of this book's failings.

In London, I must thank Richard E Kelly for setting me straight (once again) on the key elements of storytelling, and Nicole Wilkins for her tireless proofreading and suggestions. Also, my thanks to my partner, Vivian Chen, for providing the beautiful maps that accompany this book and for supporting me throughout its gestation.